GUITAR WORLD PRESENTS

VAN HALEN

EDDIE VAN HALEN. IN HIS OWN WORDS.
The inside story of the world's greatest guitarist and
his legendary band. With revealing interviews
featuring Eddie's take on Van Halen members past
and present, his guitars and his place in rock history.

From the pages of
GUITAR WORLD
magazine

Edited by
Jeff Kitts, Brad Tolinski
and Harold Steinblatt

Published by Music Content Developers, Inc.
In cooperation with Harris Publications, Inc. and Guitar World Magazine
Guitar World is a registered trademark of Harris Publications, Inc.
Exclusively Distributed by

HAL•LEONARD®
CORPORATION
7777 W. BLUEMOUND RD. P.O. BOX 13819 MILWAUKEE, WI 53213

ISBN 0-7935-8081-1
Copyright © 1997 Music Content Developers, Inc.
600 Valley Road, Suite 206, Wayne, NJ 07470

Editorial Director: Brad Tolinski
Producer: Carol Flannery
Editors: Jeff Kitts & Harold Steinblatt
Art Director: John Flannery
Cover Photo: Larry DiMarzio

Table of Contents

GUITAR WORLD, AUGUST 1992

ATOMIC PUNK

The story of how Eddie Van Halen revolutionized rock guitar.

By Dan Amrich

SOME SOUNDS ARE unmistakable. Some are undefinable. More often than not, Van Halen is both.

Today, nearly 20 years after first grabbing hold of the world's ear and shaking it violently, the aftershocks of Edward Van Halen's explosive guitar technique, radical ideas and boundless energy are still being felt. Surviving disco, punk, power pop, grunge and countless other trends, Eddie has proven himself to be the ultimate—if occasionally reluctant—rock guitar hero.

Edward Lodewijk Van Halen was born on January 26, 1957, in Nijmegen, Holland. Ten years later, he and his older brother Alex moved with their musician parents to Pasadena, California. The immigrant family had 15 dollars and a piano, an instrument Eddie set about studying diligently. But while he respected the piano, learned much about music and won numerous awards for his keyboard prowess, his heart wasn't in it. "Who wanted to sit at the piano?" he later exclaimed. "I wanted to go crazy!"

As American teens, Alex and Eddie learned both the English language and the language of rock and roll. At first, Eddie invested in a set of drums and Alex acquired a nylon-string acoustic guitar. But while Eddie was busy delivering newspapers to pay for his kit,

Alex was busy using it. Once Alex mastered "Wipeout," Eddie told Alex to keep the drums; he'd take the guitar. Both parties were happy. As Alex later recalled, "I could tell by the way he was moving his fingers around that he could do things I'd never be able to do, no matter how hard I practiced."

The things Eddie did with the guitar would ultimately change the face of rock music, but in the early days, he mostly just jammed with his brother (using a Teisco Del Rey electric guitar from Sears) and listened to a lot of early Beatles, Dave Clark Five, Jimi Hendrix, Jimmy Page and especially Eric Clapton, whose licks he learned note for note. Eventually, Eddie and Alex formed a band they called Mammoth—"a junior Cream," said Eddie—which, assisted by an endless stream of temporary bassists, played covers at high school events. Yet the more Eddie played, the more he realized he wanted to take his playing to the next level, beyond mere mimicry and into innovation.

But before anyone could hear Eddie's ideas, some basic problems had to be solved: primarily, finding a place to practice and finding cash to buy a PA system for their live gigs. Both difficulties were solved when David Lee Roth, an acquaintance from whom the Van Halens occasionally rented equipment, joined the band. Roth's dad let them practice in the basement, a crucial advantage. Once they got going, Roth's extroverted antics garnered the band a lot of attention. When Michael Anthony gave up his own band, Snake, to play bass for Mammoth in 1974, the group became the hottest ticket in Pasadena. It wasn't too long after that they realized that Mammoth was the name of another band in the area, so Roth suggested they be known simply as Van Halen. "It had power to it," he said. Nobody could come up with anything better, so it stuck.

In those early days, the band played mostly covers for five hours a night at various Southern California clubs. Before long, Eddie's skills had developed to the point where local guitarists were heading to Van Halen shows to check out his raw sound, homemade guitars and unorthodox two-hand tapping technique. Eddie, meanwhile, took his brother's advice and played solos with his back to the audience, to prevent any enterprising guitarists from ripping him off. As time wore on, the band started getting gigs at well-known L.A. clubs like the Whisky and the Starwood, and developed an original repertoire. In 1977 they impressed Kiss bassist Gene Simmons, with whose help they recorded, under the name Daddy Longlegs, a professional demo—which was promptly rejected by every major label. It wasn't until Warner Bros. producer Ted Templeman personally convinced the label's president, Mo Ostin, to see a VH show that the band got signed.

In February 1978, Van Halen's self-titled first album, produced by Templeman, was released. "Runnin' with the Devil," with its cacophonous wail of car horns, kicked the record off in grand style. But this was nothing but a warning shot, for the ensuing track, "Eruption," was pure rock guitar revolution. Pinch harmonics, hammer-ons, two-handed tapping, whammy bar dives so deep they gave listeners the bends—all conspired to introduce open-mouthed rock guitarists to the future. Edward Van Halen had personally reconfigured the technical and aural parameters of his instrument—all in one minute, 42 seconds flat.

The combined assault of "Runnin' with the Devil," a high-octane cover of the Kinks' "You Really Got Me" and Ed's spectacular guitar calisthenics helped *Van Halen* crack the Top 20 and sell two million copies in a matter of months. Opening nationwide tours for acts like Montrose and Journey, the band quickly cemented a backstage reputation for relishing babes, booze and bad behavior, spearheaded in no small part by Roth. On stage, however, Van Halen was all business, pounding out adrenaline-soaked half-hour sets for stunned audiences. By the time they arrived in Europe to open for Black Sabbath, all recognized that the changing of the heavy rock guard was imminent.

"They blew us off the stage every night," recalled Ozzy Osbourne. "It was so embarrassing. We didn't have the fire anymore. They kicked our asses, but it convinced me of two things: my days with Black Sabbath were over, and Van Halen was going to be a very successful band."

Later that year, in December, the band recorded a second album, *Van Halen II*. "Dance the Night Away" hit Number 15, holding its own against the disco fare of the time, and by June, 1979, Van Halen, with 22 tons of equipment in tow, was headlining a UK tour. Songs like "Beautiful Girls" helped solidify David Lee Roth's party persona, while the nylon-string solo on "Spanish Fly" offered proof that Ed's genius transcended his electric guitar playing.

By 1980, Van Halen had helped fuel a resurgence of heavy metal—though Eddie was uncomfortable characterizing the band in those terms. David Lee Roth, meanwhile, described Van Halen's music as "a cross between religion and hockey." In any case, the group's third album, *Women and Children First*, oozing distorted riffs and thunderous drums, ultimately hit the ninth position on the *Billboard* album chart. It also contained decidedly non-metallic gems like the acoustic "Could This Be Magic?"—the first tune to feature Eddie's slide playing.

That year, during the band's "Invasion" tour, Eddie began romancing TV actress Valerie Bertinelli, who became Mrs. Van Halen in April of 1981. Ironically, it was during this time of Eddie's great personal happiness that his band released its darkest album, *Fair Warning*. Creepy, synth-driven pieces like "Sunday Afternoon in the Park," along with "Mean Street" and "Dirty Movies," with their sordid themes, ultimately overshadowed party rockers like "Unchained" and "So This Is Love?" But despite Warner Bros.' decision to not release a single, the album still reached Number Six, charting higher than any of its predecessors.

In order to meet an April, 1982, release date set by Warner Bros., the band recorded their fifth album, *Diver Down*, in 12 days. The record clocked in at under 30 minutes and contained five cover tunes among its 12 tracks, a fact which didn't sit well with Eddie. "That's my least favorite record," he said later. "I'd rather bomb with my own songs than make it with someone else's." Still, the album isn't without its high points, particularly the volume-knob trickery of "Cathedral," the Spanish-style intro to "Little Guitars" and the guest appearance of Eddie and Alex's dad, Jan Van Halen, who played clarinet on "Big Bad Bill (is Sweet William Now)." With the album soaring to Number Three, Warner Bros. was no doubt very happy when the "Hide Your Sheep" tour kicked off at the mammoth 1982 US Festival in California.

But the tour was short, and Eddie found himself with some welcome down time at home. Unexpectedly, R&B legend Quincy Jones called and asked Eddie to contribute a solo to "Beat It," a new song slated to appear on Michael Jackson's upcoming album, *Thriller*. In the past, Van Halen members had, by mutual agreement, generally refrained from taking on outside projects. (Although Eddie had previously contributed to Nicolette Larson's *Nicolette* and Brian May's *Star Fleet Project*.) But since his bandmates were all out on vacation, Eddie agreed. Unhappy with the section Jones asked him to solo over, Van Halen requested a change; his request was granted. He subsequently cut two takes in 20 minutes. "Beat It" spent three weeks at Number One and, largely thanks to Eddie's solo, crossed over to radio stations that normally didn't play R&B artists. *Thriller* went on to become the largest-selling album of all time; Eddie, meanwhile, received a thank-you note and no payment, having done the solo as a favor.

While Roth later downplayed Eddie's achievement, the "Beat It" favor was ultimately returned by listeners when Van Halen's *1984* was released on New Year's Eve, 1983. The leadoff single, "Jump," hit Number One in late February and stayed there for five weeks—the band's only chart-topping hit to date. The fact that the guitar god's biggest hit was driven by a synthesizer hook seemed to bother everyone but Eddie; to him, it was just music. After all, the guy did have a classical piano background. Besides, the guitar faithful were rewarded with *1984*'s "Panama," "Top Jimmy" and the raucous "Hot for Teacher."

But widespread pop success came with a price. While David Lee Roth lapped up the attention, Eddie was thinking ahead to the next record. Roth had always preferred life on the road to life in a soundbooth and eventually the personal and work ethic differences between himself and Van Halen came to a head. Roth, who had tasted solo success with his *Crazy From the Heat* album, announced in June, 1995 that he was leaving the band. Ted Templeman went with him, leaving the producing duties to longtime engineer Donn Landee and the increasingly involved Eddie.

With Roth gone, the band considered recording the next album with a different lead singer on every track, but abandoned the idea after auditioning Sammy Hagar, ex-Montrose vocalist and a solo artist in his own right. Hagar's fresh energy and more agreeable personality fueled 1986's *5150*, produced by Landee, the band and Mick Jones. Despite open skepticism over the band's ability to overcome the departure of Roth, the album became the band's first Number One record, spawning two keyboard-heavy hits, "Why Can't This Be Love" and "Dreams," as well as strong guitar rockers like "Best of Both Worlds" and "Get Up." Eddie later referred to *5150* as "a very inspired record" with "a lot of soul."

The band headlined the Monsters of Rock tour in the summer of 1988, playing all-day concerts alongside Metallica and the Scorpions, and released the second Hagar-fronted record, *OU812*, in June. With fans hungry for new Van Halen material, it soared to the top of the album charts in less than a month, and sat there for four weeks. "When It's Love," "Finish What Ya Started" and "Feels So Good" all enjoyed heavy radio airplay.

After a grueling tour, the band enjoyed some well-earned R&R. In 1990, Van Halen opened their own club, the Cabo Wabo Cantina, in Cabo San Lucas, Mexico. The next year, on March 16, 1991, Eddie and Valerie gave birth to their first son, Wolfgang William Van Halen. With a different sort of partner, Eddie soon fathered another child: the Ernie Ball Music Man guitar, which he co-designed. For a tinkerer like Eddie, creating a production instrument represented the ultimate thrill. "I used to endorse the guitar I played," he said, "but I *designed* this one. It's a whole different ballgame."

Following closely behind the new axe came a new Andy Johns-produced album, *For Unlawful Carnal Knowledge*, in June, 1991. The lead single, "Poundcake," features an opening hook made by an electric drill, while "Top of the World" picks up where "Jump" left off—literally, as it uses "Jump's" outro as its opening riff. Although the piano-based "Right Now" turned into a huge hit, the album seemed more guitar-oriented than the band's most recent efforts. It stood at the Number One spot on the album charts for three weeks.

Although Eddie had in 1985 asserted that he "didn't see the purpose" of a live album, he eventually changed his mind, and *Right Here, Right Now* was released in February, 1993. The band's first 2-CD set included material from their latest tour, featuring such highlights as a bass solo, a drum solo, lots of stage chatter from Hagar and a live solo by Eddie that encompassed "Eruption," "Cathedral" and "316."

In January of 1995, not long after Eddie finally conquered his longtime battle with alcohol, Van Halen released the appropriately titled *Balance*, with tunes ranging from the commercially poppy "Can't Stop Lovin' You" to the power boogie of "Big Fat Money." Also featured were no less than three instrumentals, reportedly included because of a dispute with Hagar involving his unwillingness to write lyrics. The album continued the band's Number One streak, holding the top spot for a week.

Within six months, however, Hagar would be history, his departure triggered by internal disputes over Van Halen's planned greatest hits album and the band's contributions to the soundtrack to the film *Twister*. "We actually had problems on every album except for *5150*," Eddie subsequently revealed. With Hagar's departure, old-school fans hoped beyond hope that a reunion with David Lee Roth was in the offing—and it was, albeit for just two new songs for 1996's *Best of Volume 1*: "Me Wise Magic" and "Can't Get This Stuff No More." With "Magic" as its single, *Best Of* nailed *Billboard*'s top album spot, but almost as soon as the original lineup started feeling each other out, a disastrous backstage ego flareup at the MTV Video Music Awards squelched all hopes of future involvements between the band and the disappointed Roth. "I'll put it very simply," Eddie summed up. "Dave and Sam both suffer from L.S.D.—lead singer's disease."

Meanwhile, former Extreme vocalist Gary Cherone landed the coveted Van Halen frontman job. "Gary's very talented, and we work very, very well together," said Eddie.

As Van Halen get ready to release a new album and prepare to enter the third distinct phase of what has been a tumultuous career, their millions of fans can rest assured that no matter who's at the vocal helm, it is their brilliant guitarist that remains in control of the band's destiny. At age 41, Eddie is what he has always been: a master guitarist, supremely confident of his craft and his multiple role as songwriter, producer and musician. "I still have so much music in me," says Eddie. "So much that needs to come out."

GUITAR WORLD, JANUARY 1981

THE NEW KING OF HEAVY METAL

GUITAR WORLD kicked off its first full year of operation by interviewing the man who would change rock guitar forever.

By John Stix

"JUST GIVE ME some of that rock and roll music. Any old way you choose it. It's got a back beat you can't lose it Any old time you use it. Gotta be rock and roll music. If you want to dance with me."

Chuck Berry's ode to the music he helped make great is all right with Edward Van Halen. You might just say that, at 23, Van Halen is simply respecting his elders as he explodes in the studio and on stage with music—the music he first lovingly nurtured in his basement and later turned up to a high flame in small bars, and, ultimately, in huge arenas.

The self-described "kid living his rock and roll dream" was born near Amsterdam, Holland, where his father, a professional musician, ensured that both Edward and his brother Alex were studying piano at an early age. The young Eddie practiced the classics diligently, but even then, his was a rock and roll heart. "Who wanted to sit at the piano?" says Van Halen. "I wanted to go crazy. Everybody turned me on. I grew up on a lot of early Beatles, Dave Clark Five, Cream, Clapton, Page, Beck and Hendrix."

He was 10 when the family moved to Los Angeles, where he attended local schools. The budding guitarist played the usual course of high school dances and, upon earning his diploma, immediately set his sights on the local bar circuit. "The members of Van Halen were all in various bands in the L.A. area," he recalls. "But when we reached college age everyone else started flaking off, wanting to be doctors. We got stuck with each other." They played every dive and covered all the oldies, including a version of the Kinks' "You Really Got Me," which Eddie calls "a hot tune we turned into a jet plane."

The crowds grew in size, to the point where it was not uncommon for a Van Halen gig to draw 3,000 people. Kiss' Gene Simmons became interested in the band, and paid for their first demo sessions. Ultimately, Warner Bros. Records chairman Mo Ostin caught their act at the Starwood Club. So impressed was Ostin that he signed Van Halen the next day. The rest, of course, is hard rock history: Over the next three years, the one-time bar band metamorphosed into an arena supergroup. "I never imagined that we would get to where we are this quickly," says EVH.

Edward Van Halen is hardly the arrogant, angry young man of rock and roll lore. No embittered snarls curl his lip; he is a perpetual grinner—his smile could successfully sell bad soft drinks on television. And why not? Eddie is one happy guy.

"Everything I did was because I wanted to do it," he says straightforwardly. "If I weren't playing this arena—if I were playing a club—I'd still be doing it, because that's what I want to do. I love playing the guitar."

He not only plays guitar, he builds them. When we met for this interview he was surrounded by guitar parts, preparing to assemble instruments for a performance that was only two hours away. As the individual pickups, bridges, necks and strings became guitars, I developed a very clear image of the technician himself. This was a brilliant, young, high-voltage rock guitarist who—despite his success—remarkably is able to keep his feet on the ground.

"I'm not a rock star," says Van Halen firmly. "When kids ask me how it feels to be a rock star, I say, 'Leave me alone.' I'm not in it for the fame, I'm in it because I like to play."

GUITAR WORLD: You began as a piano student. How advanced a player did you become?

EDWARD VAN HALEN: I won first prize four years in a row at Long Beach City College for my category. The piano is a universal instrument. If you start there, learn your theory and how to read, you can go on to any other instrument.

GW: It sounds like you had a solid foundation in the basics.

VAN HALEN: Well, I'm not a good reader—I would read music and then memorize. The one thing I do have is good ears. I don't mean perfect pitch, but an ear for picking things up, which I developed through piano theory. But I never had a guitar lesson in my life, except from listening to Eric Clapton records.

GW: Do you have the ability to hear something in your head and play it instantly?

VAN HALEN: Not automatically or perfectly, but that's the thing—I don't think when I play. It's spontaneous, it's feeling. It's not calculated or worked out ahead of time. That's why you might say I play "off the wall." When I was in junior college at Pasadena City, I took a scoring and arranging class with a professor named Dr. Fischer. Frank Zappa also studied with him. Dr. Fischer was very avant garde—the one thing he taught me was to forget the rules. If it sounds good, it is good.

GW: I imagine you took to the guitar fairly easily.

VAN HALEN: Not to sound egoed out, but I was a natural. My father has been a professional musician all his life, and he told me, "Kid, you've got it." Some have got it and some don't, but even people who don't have it can practice long enough to get it down—to a point. There's always a difference between a person who has the feel and those who don't. The difference is in the amount of emotion expressed in your playing. I listened to a Debussy piece played by two different pianists, and it was like day and night. One guy had it and every note was beautiful. The other guy had lead fingers.

GW: Did you ever go through a period where you imitated others?

VAN HALEN: Definitely, and Clapton was it; I knew every note he played. That's what I was known for around home. Me, Alex, and a bass player we knew called ourselves Mammoth, and we were the junior Cream.

GW: Have you ever thought of working with another guitarist?

VAN HALEN: I've never played with another guitarist because I make enough sound on my own. What I love about Cream is that everybody had to put out. It was three people making all this noise, and you could hear each person. That Allman Brothers feel is something I never got into. Duane Allman was an excellent slide guitarist, but I never cared for Dickey Betts. I found their music too cluttered for my taste.

GW: You must have studied your instrument quite intensely in your Clapton days. Do you still work as hard to improve your playing?

VAN HALEN: Yes, but I don't call it practice. This will sound real funny to you, but we tour for eight weeks and then take eight days off. When I'm home on a break, I lock myself in my room and play guitar. After two or three hours I start getting into this total meditation. It's a feeling I think few people experience. It's usually then that I come up with weird stuff. It just flows. I can't force myself. I don't sit down and say, "I've got to practice."

GW: In what ways have you improved since the first album was released?

VAN HALEN: I don't consider myself a better player—I consider myself different. With my technical ability, I can play just about as fast as I'd like to play. Any faster at the volume I play and I'd have distortion. So on a technical level there's no reason to get any faster.

GW: But do you still reach any new plateaus?

VAN HALEN: Sure I do.

GW: Can you point to some that have appeared on your records?

VAN HALEN: The solo on "And the Cradle Will Rock" [*Women and Children First*] is different. I do one short lick on "Cradle" that is very spontaneous. It came out because I've been listening to Allan

Holdsworth, who I think is the baddest. On the second album I expanded a little more on harmonics.

GW: You're referring to the technique of producing false harmonics by using your right hand on the fretboard?

VAN HALEN: Yes. I discovered that while using my right-hand first finger to tap, I could also use the same finger to create harmonics by hitting the fret an octave above where my left hand was positioned. I'm starting to expand on that by using all the harmonics within the octave. I also use the slap technique, which I got from black bass players.

I owe the way I hold the pick when I tap to Jimi Hendrix. I saw a movie that showed Jimi "palming" his pick by holding it between the joints of his middle finger. I pick weird, too: I use the thumb and the middle finger.

GW: It's interesting that you don't play overly long guitar solos in your songs.

VAN HALEN: I haven't heard anyone do an interesting long guitar solo outside of early Clapton. In the live show, I do a guitar solo that is long; some people may think it's boring, but I have fun. Clapton was my favorite. With his feel, he'd hit one note where someone else would hit 20, and it would really do something to you, whereas another person's 20 would leave you flat.

GW: You could be accused of playing too many notes.

VAN HALEN: I'm not Eric Clapton. I might play fast, but there are a lot of people who play fast with no feel at all. I'm high-energy, but I think I combine a little more feeling and some different techniques than other high-energy players.

GW: What do you think of other "high-energy" players around, like Joe Perry, Ted Nugent and Jimmy Page?

VAN HALEN: I hate doing this because you're going to make me come off like an asshole. Enough people hate me already.

GW: Do you like Joe Perry?

VAN HALEN: I don't like him because I don't think he likes me. I met him once. I walked up to shake his hand, and he looked at me and walked away. As a guitarist I don't think he's that good. He lacks feel.

GW: What about Ted Nugent?

VAN HALEN: Nugent is a very nice guy, but I don't really like his tone.

GW: And Jimmy Page?

VAN HALEN: Jimmy Page is an excellent producer. *Led Zeppelin I* and *II* are classics. As a player he's very good in the studio, but I've never seen him play well live. He's sloppy. He plays like he's got a broken hand and he's two years old. If you put out a good album and play like a two-year old, what's the purpose?

GW: Have you ever thought of the possibility of yourself joining the ranks of greats like Clapton, Page and Beck?

VAN HALEN: It's very hard to say. That's like saying I'm the best, and I can't say that. I'm not. I can't say I'm going to influence people, but I know a lot of people who are using their right hand on the fingerboard who never did it before.

GW: Would you like to be thought of as a great player?

VAN HALEN: I'd just like people to like what I play. I don't want people to say, "You're number one." It's a matter of taste. To me, Allan Holdsworth is number one. Kids might listen to him and not even understand what he's doing. Older people might think I suck.

GW: What about your quieter side?

VAN HALEN: There's a lot you haven't heard. I had more of an acoustic intro to "In a Simple Rhyme," but we didn't do it because everyone would immediately say, "He's pulling a Zeppelin." We did "Could This Be Magic?" but it's a joke.

GW: Have you started thinking about a fourth album?

VAN HALEN: I've got a load of ideas, but we don't know what we're going to do until we walk into that studio. What we do is tour for 10 months, come home, go to the basement and make songs out of the ideas we've accumulated while out on the road. We invite Ted [*Templeman, Van Halen producer*] down, and he picks what he likes. We argue a bit, compromise, and we usually have a final say on which material gets recorded. We spend a week rehearsing in the basement, and go straight to the studio.

GW: Sounds like you like to work quickly.

VAN HALEN: *Women and Children First* took only four days for the music and six days for the vocals. "Dance the Night Away" [*Van Halen II*] was written on the spot, in the studio. I never played slide guitar before "Could This Be Magic?" I had something totally different in mind for the song, but Ted said, "Try playing slide." I did it right there on the spot, and that was it. "Cradle Will Rock" was a first take—a bunch of songs were first takes. We don't go for perfection, we just go for spirit. There are mistakes, but I'm happy with everything on our records. That's not to say we won't play things differently when we perform live.

GW: Do you prefer live work or recording?

VAN HALEN: Performing, of course! I play for self-satisfaction, but it makes it even better when other people enjoy it.

GW: How did you learn to build guitars?

VAN HALEN: Trial and error. I've ruined many guitars. I ruined a beautiful old Gibson ES-335 while I was learning to re-fret, but I've really become a pro since then.

GW: Do you ever build them from scratch?

VAN HALEN: Sometimes. The natural wood instrument was a very rough cut that I jigsawed out, contoured and fretted. My main guitar, the red one, used to be a Charvel copy of a Strat. A long time ago I used a '59 Strat. But the single pickup hummed too much and it sounded thin unless I used a fuzz box or something. After using the 335, I tried the Strat again and thought, "Why don't I cut my own pickguard and put a humbucker in it?" It worked, except Fender wood isn't as dense as I'd like. The Charvel is made of ash, which is a little denser. It was my idea to rear-load it.

GW: What kind of pickups do you use?

VAN HALEN: I use Gibson PAFs, DiMarzios and Seymour Duncans. I'd say that out of all the super distortion garbage out there, I like Seymour Duncan best. It's a matter of taste. I prefer old PAFs because they get the tone I like.

GW: What about necks?

VAN HALEN: I always use unfinished maple necks because I like to feel the wood. They're made by Lynn Ellsworth at Boogie Body in Seattle, Washington.

GW: Why only one pickup and volume control?

VAN HALEN: In order for me to get the front pickup to sound the way I like, the back one would sound like crap.

GW: Your tuning pegs are made by Schaller, but your nut and bridge piece look like custom gear. I've never seen anyone cut off the ball of the string before running it through the bridge.

VAN HALEN: The nut and bridge are made by Floyd Rose. I use them for performing only—I don't use them in the studio because they're too bright-sounding for me. So I use the same guitar but with a different neck, a different PAF and a Fender bridge. I needed to have the guitar like this because we tune a little differently than most people. We use the Peterson Strobe Tuner (Model 420) to tune down a step and a quarter. You do lose something; the guitar was made to be tuned to an A-440. When you start taking away from that, you lose harmonic overtones and get more slack in the strings. The only thing about the Floyd stuff is that if you break a string, the whole thing goes out of whack.

GW: What about your "snake" guitar—who dreamed that up?

VAN HALEN: A friend of mine, John Sterry, came up with the idea. It used to be an Explorer. The neck and body are of the rarest wood you can buy—Carina wood from Africa.

GW: Are particular amplifiers important to you?

VAN HALEN: Very important. I don't use any kind of preamp distortion—I go for total tube distortion. I have Mark II Marshalls, which I've changed back to tubes. In the studio I use my old baby 100-watt Super Leads with Marshall bottoms.

GW: Do you use any outboard gear?

VAN HALEN: My equipment is probably more primitive than what most people use. My pedal board is a piece of plywood with an MXR Phase 90, an Echo-Plex and an MXR Flanger. Ted Nugent laughed his ass off when he saw it the first time. I like making different sounds by using different techniques, as opposed to pedals.

Neil Zlozower

GUITAR WORLD, JULY 1985

THE LIFE AND TIMES OF VAN HALEN

As "Jump" hit BILLBOARD's Number One slot, GUITAR WORLD presented one of the first interviews from 5150, Edward's new home studio.

By Steven Rosen

EDWARD VAN HALEN, born in Nijmegen, the Netherlands, on January 26, 1957, has been disseminating what he calls "the brown sound" now for over six years, or since the Pasadena quartet released its self-titled debut album. *Van Halen* sold over two million copies, with every subsequent release—*Van Halen II, Women and Children First, Fair Warning, Diver Down* and *1984*—selling well in excess of one million units. *1984* finished sixth on *Billboard*'s Top Albums of 1984; the "Jump" single ranked sixth as well, after occupying the coveted Number One position for a time.

1984 is the first album recorded at Edward's 16-track home studio, 5150 (a name derived from an L.A. police code for the criminally insane). The cohesive batch of songs on the album re-establishes the balance and atmosphere which were notably absent from the group's *Diver Down* effort. Edward also establishes himself as a formidable synthesist on such tracks as the title song, "I'll Wait," and, of course, "Jump."

Coming off yet another world tour, Edward recently set aside several days to discuss *1984*, and the music he made prior to this breakthrough sixth album. Most of the conversations took place at 5150, amid scattered guitars, reels of two-inch tape and empty beer cans. Rarely was the studio phone silent for more than an hour during our time together; it was during the unlikely lapses that much of the following interview took place.

Edward's schedule, even by a musician's standards, is a severe one. He ordinarily works from early evening to well past noon, experimenting with new guitars, programming rhythms on his LinnDrum and working on bits and pieces of music stashed on hundreds of scattered cassettes. "Noodling," he calls it.

Van Halen is wary of interviews—and interviewers—but quite adept at fielding questions. He is deliberate with his responses, and refreshingly forthright. As a result, what follows is a genuinely intimate look at the guitarist who, more than anyone since the golden days of the late Sixties, has redefined the limits of the electric six-string.

Eddie Van Halen's character hasn't changed. He is truly taken aback by compliments. Despite his enormous success, he is the same self-effacing man he was years ago, when the Van Halen group first signed with Warner Bros.

Here, then, is Edward Van Halen—father of the "brown sound."

GUITAR WORLD: 1984 was a productive year for Van Halen.
EDWARD VAN HALEN: The best year we've had. We started to see not just success, but also the satisfaction of knowing what we can accomplish. It was a strong year in every aspect.
GW: Do you think it's the best music you've made?
VAN HALEN: That's hard to say. I like everything we've done.
GW: Did you think the *1984* album would be so well-received?
VAN HALEN: I figured that it was good and would get noticed. But how can anyone say, "This is going to go platinum?"
GW: Are you the final arbiter of what eventually makes it on record?

VAN HALEN: I'm not the only one involved. If the rest of the guys don't like something, I'm out-voted. But with regard to my happiness about something we've recorded, what I think of it is more important. If I like it and other people don't, of course my reaction might be, "Why don't they like it?" But I don't write to please other people. It's nice, but you have to please yourself first.

GW: You've written songs that never made their way to vinyl.

VAN HALEN: That's because Ted [*Templeman, Van Halen producer*] or somebody in the band voted against it, and decided it wasn't right for that point in time. "House of Pain" [*1984*] was written before we were signed. A lot of things I write aren't accepted with open arms, whether it's because of the instrumentation or that they just don't like the music.

GW: What if you feel very strongly about a particular song?

VAN HALEN: "I'll Wait" [*1984*] was one. Donn [*Landee, Edward's engineer*] and I both felt very strongly about it. Nobody else did, so we put it down ourselves. Then they heard it and said [*in dumb-struck tone*], "Uh, what's that?" I'm not going to sit there and cry if they don't like it, but sometimes something gets lost in the translation of an idea.

GW: Does that happen very often?

VAN HALEN: Obviously, it happens a lot. But the thing is, when you put it down on tape and they still don't like it, then there isn't a whole lot of room for miscommunication.

GW: Do you think the difference in musical tastes between you and David Lee Roth has made Van Halen what it is?

VAN HALEN: I'm sure that has had something to do with it, but it's not necessarily just Dave. It's Al and Ted and Donn and me all having different musical tastes. But it's not even musical tastes. Music is music, and if something is good and you like it, it's good. I like some jazz, I like some punk. Dave and Al listen to just about everything.

GW: Do you bounce ideas off [*bassist*] Mike Anthony?

VAN HALEN: I show my ideas to him along with everyone else. He generally goes along with the majority and usually doesn't have any strong preferences.

GW: How close is the final version of a song to the original demo?

VAN HALEN: Generally, there isn't much rewriting. Parts might be rearranged or chopped here and there.

GW: Does Ted help with these arrangements?

VAN HALEN: [*pauses*] Yes and no. He has a talent that, in a way, is unbeatable. But sometimes he doesn't allow other ideas to develop before he puts his this-is-the-way-to-go thing to it. And that's not putting him down at all. You can't expect any two people to think and feel identically about an idea. But that's how ideas get totally twisted and distorted from the original seed: People get involved in how they think it should sound. And I'm sure I'm as guilty of this as Ted and Al and Dave and everyone put together.

GW: Where would you be if you had never gotten involved with Ted Templeman?

VAN HALEN: I think we'd be where we are. But Ted tends to look for singles, or songs that could be a single for radio play; that's his way of thinking. We think differently. Period. I think we definitely complement him and vice-versa. Both parties would be different without the other. It's hard to say whether it would be better or worse. I think the reason we sound different is that the individuals in the band have their own styles.

GW: Van Halen seems to be the yardstick by which every other rock band is measured. Do you think that's because you write great songs?

VAN HALEN: What's a great song? Lots of people think a song without singing is not a song. Tell that to Beethoven and he'll kick your ass.

GW: Would you like to have been Beethoven?

VAN HALEN: I wouldn't want to have died at the age he did [57]. Anyone who wouldn't want to be as respected as he is would be a fool. I'm happy being who I am—I wouldn't want to be anybody else.

GW: How would you say your songwriting has grown?

VAN HALEN: It just changes. I guess, if I look back, I am better because I've been doing it longer. Or maybe it's easier. I'm more comfortable, more at ease constructing a song. But coming up with the ideas is just as difficult. That's why I say I don't know if I've grown.

GW: But you probably have a better understanding of when the structure is right.

VAN HALEN: Probably, yeah, but that's like saying, "Yes, I've been conditioned."

GW: No, it's just that you're learning the craft.

VAN HALEN: Yeah, but who's to say what's right? It's all within yourself—and, I guess, within myself I've gotten a better handle on what I feel is right.

GW: When did you first start writing?

VAN HALEN: I've probably been coming up with riffs ever since I picked up an instrument. It was probably around the time I played high school dances. Just to back up a bit, a main element you're leaving out in my own songwriting is Donn Landee. Donn and I work together at structuring things—I bounce everything off of him before anyone hears it.

GW: So had Donn not been part of the picture from the beginning, Van Halen's sound might have been different?

VAN HALEN: Definitely. And it would be harder.

GW: Donn understands you pretty well.

VAN HALEN: You said what I was trying to say. We understand each other well. To the point where the way he makes things sound is basically the way I hear things in my head. This is very unusual.

GW: So what the public hears on the tape is the guitar sound you heard in your head?

VAN HALEN: Within each given song. I can't say every record was exact. But I'm happy with everything on the last album [*1984*], and Donn and I worked very much as one on that. We're proud of it because it's something we felt was an accurate representation of what we were capable of. That goes for the band as a whole, too. But it was Donn's and my baby.

GW: You haven't really written lyrics to any extent.

VAN HALEN: It's not something I'm good at, or something I've spent any time with. A lot of times the way people write lyrics is so personal that nobody knows what the hell the words mean. Dave is that way. I don't even know the lyrics to our own songs, and it's no joke. Because a lot of the stuff is Dave's interpretation of life at that given moment. And even if he experienced it, it doesn't click concerning my life or the state of the nation. [*laughs*]

GW: When you write the music, you must have some idea of what the song should say, lyrically.

VAN HALEN: I never suggest to Dave what to write the lyrics about. Once he writes lyrics, Ted and Al and I suggest going this way or that way with it. I guess that's why sometimes I don't lean towards his lyrics, because something about them takes away from the mood the music creates, even covers that mood. It might take it to a better place—and sometimes not. Sometimes it takes away from the original feel of what is happening. And I can't exactly say, "Hey, it was sexy before and it isn't now." It's a feeling. Like, how do you explain [*sings opening notes of Beethoven's Fifth Symphony*]? What words would you say to that? When something sounds a certain way, I can't easily picture lyrics with it. Because it's pretty self-explanatory.

GW: Like the opening to "1984"?

VAN HALEN: Yeah; I couldn't hear any singing over that.

GW: Is a lot of the music you listen to instrumental?

VAN HALEN: Yeah, but I haven't listened to any of that stuff for at least a year. I don't even have a turntable or a cassette machine in the house.

GW: Do you draw any inspiration from modern music?

VAN HALEN: Let me put it this way: A lot of contemporary music wouldn't amount to much without lyrics. But I've seen a lot of lyrics and vocals ruin good music, in the same way opera singing over good classical music can do a heavy duty waste number on it. And who in the hell understands what they're saying in opera music? And how does someone in Japan, even though they may learn English in school, know what a person is saying? It's more the feeling. I'm not against vocals or lyrics; it's just a lot of times they rub me wrong.

GW: Do you suggest vocal melodies?

VAN HALEN: I try and help, yeah. Lines here and there. I never say, "Here's the music. Here's the melody. Fit words to these notes." Because that would be really ridiculous to say. Dave has done some stuff with the music that has been handed to him that has blown me away. Because some of the stuff I come up with is pretty twisted. Seriously. Twisted to the point where if he can squeeze a word or two in there or anywhere, he's got my vote. [*laughs*]

GW: What are your feelings about Dave's solo album?

VAN HALEN: I think it's something he always wanted to do. I think it's great he's actually doing it. Put it this way—it's something I've always wanted to do, and haven't done. I guess, in a funny way, it explains Dave as a vocalist and lyricist. He did four cover tunes— "California Girls," "Easy Street," "Just a Gigolo" and one other one— yet managed to project his personality through them. I expect it to be accepted by people in the same way everything we've done has been. I've heard it all and it sounds real good. Edgar Winter played a lot of stuff on it, and one of the Beach Boys actually sang on "California Girls." Ted produced it. It's Dave.

GW: Did Dave want any of your input?

VAN HALEN: No. It's something he wanted to do alone. He actually started doing it when Donn and I were doing the film soundtrack for *The Wild Life*. It's not that he didn't want it, but what's a solo project if you're going to have your band playing on it?

GW: Do you think Dave wanted to have some original songs?

VAN HALEN: Yeah, I guess. You'd have to ask him that, to tell you the truth. I think these were tunes that Dave feels a part of and always liked and wanted to redo. I don't think he's out to prove anything. I know it will be good for him personally and his own self-satisfaction when it takes off the way I expect and hope it will. I seriously want the best for it, in the same way he'd want the best for me or Al or Mike if we did anything outside the band.

GW: What are your solo plans?

VAN HALEN: I don't have any plans.

GW: Certainly there must be a record in you that wants to come out.

VAN HALEN: I'd say there are a few. I haven't thought about it enough or talked to Donn about it enough. I guess in a way I look at it as something Donn and I could do whenever. It's not like something we feel we have to do in order to show anything, or for any other purpose. If the band decided to take a year off, then I could do it.

But I don't want the band to take a year off because I'm doing it.

GW: Speaking of vocals, weren't you the band's singer before Dave joined?

VAN HALEN: Oh, yeah.

GW: Is that when you were known as the Broken Combs?

VAN HALEN: Broken Combs was the very first. Alex played saxophone and I played piano. This was in fourth or fifth grade. We actually had some original tunes, too. One called "Rumpus" and one called "Boogie Booger."

GW: So you've been playing with Alex since day one?

VAN HALEN: He's the only one I've ever played with, really.

GW: Was there any competition between the two of you?

VAN HALEN: No. What I couldn't do he made up for, and what he couldn't do I made up for. That's how he started playing drums. I used to play drums and he'd play 'em better, so I said, "Go ahead, you play 'em if you can do it better." I wasn't going to waste my time proving to my own brother that I could do it better.

GW: Did you play violin?

VAN HALEN: Yeah, for about three years. Al did, too. That was at the end of elementary school and the beginning of junior high. It was school-based stuff. Al actually made All City Orchestra on violin. I never did.

GW: Did you find it difficult?

VAN HALEN: I didn't like playing the songs they made me play, so I just started messing around with it and lost interest.

GW: So from the outset, you never followed the rules.

VAN HALEN: It seems that I didn't. But it wasn't intentional. I remember sitting there, pluckin' on the violin and playing along with the *Peter Gunn* series on TV.

GW: Did your father want you to play violin or piano, as opposed to guitar?

VAN HALEN: It's hard to say exactly what he wanted us to be; he wanted us just to be successful in life. Deep down he wanted it to be music. He wanted it to be piano, only to the extent that piano is the springboard to ear training—you can orchestrate your fingertips. Each finger is a different instrument. I've learned a lot from piano, and I play it more now than I have because I can play it the way I want to. No one is looking over my shoulder and saying, "No, that's wrong."

GW: You had actual piano training?

VAN HALEN: Yeah, from age six to 12. I was good. I actually won three First Prize trophies at Long Beach City College for my category in an annual contest. You sit there and practice one tune for the whole year, and they put you in a category and judge you. I think I won First Place twice and Second Place the last time, which kind of showed I was losing interest. [*laughs*]

GW: Did the feeling you had when you won First Place mean anything to you?

VAN HALEN: It didn't motivate me. After I played in the first contest, I sat in the bleachers while they held this beauty pageant countdown; I won and didn't even hear the guy say my name. So I just sat there and they passed by my category because they couldn't find me. And finally, after the recap, they said, "Is Edward Van Halen here?" and I said, "What?" I guess the only thing it really did to me was make me more nervous for the next time. I didn't expect to win or lose. It wasn't like, "Wow, I won. I'm good!" It wasn't a motivation of any kind. I don't see why I won, to tell you the truth.

GW: Did the piano training transfer itself to the guitar?

VAN HALEN: Oh, definitely, but in a very subliminal way. Because I never learned how to read, really. I used to fool the teacher. I did it all by ear.

GW: It wasn't important to you, to learn how to read?

VAN HALEN: I guess the reason it didn't get me off in any way was that all it's good for is to learn how to play songs that have been written. And I told you the reason I didn't like violin was that I didn't like the songs we were supposed to play. I guess I was just a snot-nosed kid, and I didn't want to waste the time doing it. I'm sure I could have benefited from it, somehow. I can read, I know what the notes are, but I can't sight read like Al can. He can open up anything and start playing. I never got close to that. I had to sit there and figure out the left-hand chord and I couldn't handle all those notes.

GW: Was there much music in your house?

VAN HALEN: Yeah, by my dad. In Holland I went with him when he used to play, but I was so young I don't remember. It wasn't the classical stuff then; he did that before he met my mother.

GW: Your dad supported himself as a musician?

VAN HALEN: Oh, yeah. As a matter of fact it was the only thing that pulled him through out here when we showed up in this country. We had $25 and a piano.

GW: Did your dad make records?

VAN HALEN: Yeah. I don't know exactly in what orchestra, but it wasn't "Blah blah blah featuring Jan Van Halen." It was a Philharmonic-type thing, and I have pictures of him standing up and soloing. He's probably on more records than I know.

GW: Was your mom musical?

VAN HALEN: Not professionally, but around the holidays my mom and dad jam. My mother has this huge organ with a rhythm box in it, and my dad whips out a sax and they play oldies.

GW: Did your dad push you in that direction?

VAN HALEN: No, he never discouraged us, but he didn't encourage us, either. I wanted to start playing saxophone, and I kind of felt he didn't want to spend the time. He struck me as being as impatient as I am when it comes to teaching someone something that is very difficult to teach. I don't mean the actual instrument, I mean the feeling behind it. My dad is into that so much that he doesn't even look at sax as an instrument of technical skills—it's secondary to the emotion involved.

GW: How old were you when you got your first guitar?

VAN HALEN: About 12 or 13. It was a flamenco Spanish guitar, but I didn't really consider it *my* guitar. It was Alex's, and he took classical guitar lessons while I banged away on the drums. I got left with his guitar when he started playing the drums, and decided to get an electric. It was a four-pickup $110 Teisco Del Ray from Sears. I liked it because it had the most pickups. It was fun.

GW: Did you feel anything special when you picked up the electric for the first time?

VAN HALEN: No, no message from God or anything. I thought it was neat. Some things were easy, some things were hard. I didn't even think about whether it was easy or hard; it was something I wanted to do, to have fun and feel good about doing it. Whether it took me a week to learn half a song or one day to learn five songs, I never thought of it that way.

GW: Did you get an amplifier, too?

VAN HALEN: I had an amp that was homemade by a friend of my dad's. The plug needed an adapter because it was a phono-plug. I got this weird adapter at Radio Shack and plugged my normal guitar cord into it, and turned the thing all the way up. It made a lot of noise and I started playing it while it was making all that noise. I remember Al walking in and going, "That sounds neat, man, what is that?" It was right around the time of that song, "Blues Theme" [*instrumental by the Arrows*]. Al said, "Play that," and it sounded identical. It was crappin' out, distorted, nasty, so I guess that was my first exposure to that grungy noise.

GW: When did you become aware of guitarists like Page, Beck and Clapton?

VAN HALEN: I remember hearing Jimmy Page when a friend brought over the first Led Zeppelin album. And I tripped on it. I might have actually heard that before I heard Cream. My listening history is disjointed to me. I think I might have gotten into Cream, and then dug back to find the Bluesbreakers. I got into blues for a while and then went back to Cream. It wasn't that I was into blues and followed Clapton. I just knew I really dug him and then dug back and really got into a blues kick for six or eight months, or a year. Just jamming with guys, not really playing any songs, but jamming for hours on end, playing the same progression. Fallin' down the stairs and landing on your feet.

GW: Your technique and style were developing here?

VAN HALEN: Yeah, but it was just fun to do. I didn't think, "If I do this for a year, I'll know this side of it." It was just a very natural thing; I wasn't doing anything for any purpose.

GW: Did you say to yourself at this point, "I want to be a musician"?

VAN HALEN: I have to think about when that was. I was still in junior high, so I wasn't the rebellious one—yet. Actually, I wasn't that rebellious anyway. I just managed to get myself into trouble without having to be rebellious. I never could get over how my friends could get away with murder and I was the only one to ever get caught at doing nothing.

GW: What about the story of the time you were caught looking at the exam answers?

VAN HALEN: Oh, yeah. Actually, I think Al was the one who told me about this, and I tried it and got caught. This English teacher, who was the only teacher I can remember who smoked, would leave the class during a test period and go off to the teachers' lounge and have a cigarette and my friends would go up to her desk and change grades. And I said, "Hell, I might as well do it, too." And right when I'm doing it the teacher walks in. Got nailed.

GW: Did bands like Mammoth come together while you where in high school?

VAN HALEN: Yeah, ninth, tenth grade. Genesis was another band during that time. Then there was the Trojan Rubber Company. We also used to be called the Space Brothers. When we began playing high school dances and parties we had a hell of a reputation. This is funny because Al, Donn and I were just talking about this the other day—how it seems that only since Dave has been in the band did we get this rowdy and crazy brown cloud hanging over us. But we had it way before Dave was even in the band. Schools wouldn't hire us, nobody wanted anything to do with us, so we had to change the name of the band to Space Brothers, just so we could play these gigs at a Catholic school.

GW: What kinds of songs did you play?

VAN HALEN: You name it: Grand Funk, Black Sabbath, Deep Purple, Cream...

GW: Was Gazarri's [*a local Hollywood club*] your first semi-professional gig?

VAN HALEN: It was a breakthrough, yes. You know I got kicked out of clubs because I played too psychedelic.

GW: You even had problems getting *into* Gazarri's.

VAN HALEN: Oh, yeah! We had to audition there at least three or four times. A guy would come running up in the middle of a song because I was too loud. But I didn't play that loud deliberately; the amp only sounded like an amp if it was all the way up. So I did everything— from keeping the plastic cover on it, to facing it against the walls, to putting Styrofoam padding in front of the speakers.

GW: Were you playing the homemade, one-pickup guitar at this point?

VAN HALEN: Not right in the beginning. I used to play a Les Paul and a 335, or whatever guitar I had at the time. I also played a Les Paul Junior. That was around the time I got a Strat and the guys didn't like it—"Sounds too thin." I said, "Okay, I'll take care of that." I slapped a humbucker in there and figured out how to wire up the rest of the stuff.

GW: So the idea for putting a humbucker in a Stratocaster body came about as a matter of necessity?

VAN HALEN: Oh, yeah. I just chiseled a hole in the body. I think I might even have some footage from the Whisky, where I played that original Fender Strat. It isn't the same one that appears on the first album. It's when I realized, "Hey, this is neat," and got one from Charvel that was actually a Linn Ellsworth guitar.

GW: Had you seen or heard anyone re-working guitars like this?

VAN HALEN: No. I hadn't really seen or heard anyone taking any time to try keeping a vibrato bar in tune either. A friend brought over a bootleg album of Hendrix in concert where he'd grab the bar, and the rest of the night it was out of tune. It was important for me, because for a long time before the Floyd Rose was developed I used a regular Fender vibrato. If you see the guitar on the first album cover [*Van Halen*], there's no Floyd Rose. I actually did the first world tour with that guitar.

GW: How did you keep it in tune?

VAN HALEN: That's a tough one to explain. Due to the tension between the nut and the tuning peg, if you bring the angle of the string down it gets stuck in the nut. So I got a brass nut with extra big grooves and no string retainers, and I used to stick the string into the Schallers and wind it upwards so the angle would be straight. I'd oil the brass nut, stick the string through the body, wind it a few times and then turn the ball end of the string, because when you tighten a string, you get tension along the string itself. I'd turn the ball so it was straight. That was just another thing in my mind that could cause a rubber band effect—where you loosen a string and it wouldn't come back to where it was. It's hard to say how much any of this had to do with it because certain strings would still go out of tune—they'd go sharp because they'd get caught up somewhere. So you'd have to go and snap it back before you hit the next chord. The thing is, I never hit all six strings when I play a chord; I'm usually doing some take-off on a chord, somehow.

I did this other thing once with a 335. They used to have a real cheap spring metal—bending vibrato on them; SGs had it too. I sawed my 335 in half because I figured I could always land on my feet and make it through a song barre-chording with the low E, A and D strings. So when I hit the vibrato bar it would only be for the high E, B and G strings. It worked great, it was neat. The three high strings would always be out of tune, and the low ones would always be in so I could always chord my way through, somehow. But the guys thought the 335 looked like something Johnny Rivers would play. I actually did that before I got a Strat. I did everything to that 335—belt-sanded it, repainted it, refretted it.

GW: When you changed from the Gibson to the Fender, did your style alter?

VAN HALEN: I never understood that. What's the difference? One less fret? I can get used to anything. I remember when I got a Strat, everyone was saying, "Oh, going to make it hard on yourself, huh?" Because people like Blackmore would say things like, "I play a Fender because it's not the pussy way, it's not easy to play." I made it as easy as a Gibson to play. I never understood why Fenders are harder to play, except possibly that the string length is longer. I never tuned standard anyway, so that relieved a little tension. Try to play to the first record. We tune to A—or somewhere around there. I never tuned; if you can find a strobe-tuner in this studio, I'll give you anything you want out of here. I'd just pick up the guitar, and whatever it was tuned to, I'd just tune the instrument to itself and have Mike tune to me, and we'd tune the synthesizer to it. Who made up the rule that an A string had to vibrate at 440, or whatever?

GW: Who made the body of your first guitar?

VAN HALEN: Boogie. I painted it almost immediately, because it was a wooden body, no finish. It was a junky, piece-of-shit body on the bottom of a stack of other bodies. It was a second. I gave the guy $50 and got a [Boogie] neck for $80. I picked up the body and neck and slapped it together; it's not that difficult.

GW: What kind of guitar sound did you hear?

VAN HALEN: I guess a cross between a Gibson and a Fender—a humbucker sound with a vibrato. Bigsbys were totally childish things. You couldn't really use them to bend pitches; they were a vibrato type of thing. What I wanted to do was fall off the edge of buildings.

GW: Did you install Gibson frets?

VAN HALEN: Yeah. I got the fret wire from Linn Ellsworth and slapped them in. He told me how to do it. A couple popped up here and there so I got out the Krazy Glue.

GW: Do you remember the first time you played the guitar after it was assembled?

VAN HALEN: Yeah, it was neat. I thought, "You can't buy one of these!" I felt like I was onto something, and obviously I was.

GW: Why just one pickup?

VAN HALEN: In a two-humbucker-style Gibson, in order to get a clean, bright front pickup [*neck position*] sound, you'd have to sacrifice the sound of the rear pickup. I couldn't get what I wanted out of the front pickup, and I didn't feel like compromising, so I tended to stick with the rear one. And I tried to make up for a different sound color with playing techniques.

GW: You used this guitar for the first tour?

VAN HALEN: Before the first tour—during the Starwood and Whisky days. That was a couple of years before the first album.

GW: Had you always used Marshalls?

VAN HALEN: I tended to blow them up, so I used an old white Bassman or Bandmaster through a Marshall cabinet. I can't remember.

GW: Were you using pedals?

VAN HALEN: Same thing as on the first three tours: MXR flanger, MXR phaser and an Echoplex.

GW: What was that hollowed-out bombshell you had on stage?

VAN HALEN: That's what I used for the tail end of "Eruption." It was a Univox echo chamber. It had a miniature eight-track cassette in it, and the way it would adjust the rate of repeat was by the speed of the motor, and not by tape heads. So if you recorded something on the tape, the faster you played the motor back the faster it would repeat. And vice versa. I liked some of the noises I got out of them, but their motors would always burn out. I don't know how many broken ones I have. Then they stopped making them.

GW: What were the first tours like?

VAN HALEN: We went out with Sabbath, Ronnie Montrose, Journey. We did "A Day on the Green" [*in Oakland*] with everyone from AC/DC to Foreigner. It was a hell of an experience.

GW: Were you playing well then, by your own standards?

VAN HALEN: Yeah, I think so. I wasn't ashamed of my playing. I didn't feel I had a lot to learn. I had a lot to learn about dealing with people, but I felt we held our ground pretty well. If anything, we took a little too much ground. Unintentionally. We didn't think, "Hey, we're the best." We just did our gig and whatever happened, happened. Everyone else was a victim of his own bullshit. It didn't come from us.

GW: What was it like, recording the first album?

VAN HALEN: We didn't have a whole lot to say about much of anything. The songs basically got recorded the way we played 'em. Very few overdubs. I guess it was Ted's idea to make it come off as pure and simple and honest as it was live.

GW: Did you agree with that?

VAN HALEN: I wasn't sure. By the time Donn got through with it, I really liked it. I didn't know what making a record was. I guess it was good that we did approach it that way, because when we played live, you were only going to get more.

GW: Did the songs on the first album mirror what you'd been playing live?

VAN HALEN: Yeah. Things like "Ain't Talkin' 'Bout Love" and "Jamie's Cryin' " weren't on the original demo.

GW: Had you been playing "Eruption" live?

VAN HALEN: Yeah. Ted heard me practicing it for a Whisky show while I was waiting and he asked, "What's that?" I just didn't think it would be something we'd put on a record. He liked it, Donn liked it, and everyone else agreed that we should throw it on. I played it two or three times for the record, and we kept the one which seemed to flow. I like the way it sounds; I've never heard a guitar sound like it. It's not that my playing was so great, it just sounds like some classical instrument. Donn really made it sound like more than it is, in a way.

GW: Were there any other songs you recorded which didn't make it on *Van Halen*?

VAN HALEN: "Loss of Control," which ended up on *Women and Children First*. We wrote "Loss of Control" and "Ain't Talkin' 'Bout Love" at the same time; we were actually making fun of punk rockers. "Ain't Talkin' 'Bout Love" was actually a stupid thing to us, just two chords. It didn't end up sounding punk, but that was the intention.

GW: I suppose "Loss of Control" wouldn't have fit on the first record. It was pretty different.

VAN HALEN: [*laughs*] You said it, not me!

GW: Had you been in a studio prior to the first album?

VAN HALEN: We were in the studio once before, with [*Kiss bassist*] Gene Simmons. That was about a year before.

GW: What did you learn from that experience?

VAN HALEN: I learned that I didn't like overdubbing. Gene naturally assumed I knew that was how it's done. Ordinarily, I would noodle between chord lines, and I had to fill in those rhythm spots on

Neil Zlozower

the tape. And I'd say, "Oh, I can't do that, I have to stick to this." So it was rather uncomfortable. When we got in the studio with Ted and Donn, I asked them if it would be okay to play the way I do live. And they said, "Sure, make it easier for all of us."

GW: Prior to going into the studio with him, had you heard any of Ted's work?

VAN HALEN: The first Montrose album; that was about it. Before we went into the studio to do the first album, we did a demo tape for Warner Bros. with Ted and Donn. There were 30 songs on it, and afterwards we picked songs from those for the first album. We did the 30 songs in one day, and the next day, Dave, Mike and I put down the vocals. But after we did that demo tape we came up with other songs, like "Ain't Talkin' 'Bout Love." So since we'd done a demo tape, it was easy doing the record because it was the same set-up and same way of recording. As a matter of fact, we have a bunch of songs from that tape we still haven't done. But they were written then, and I think I write better now. "House of Pain" was on that tape, and that just ended up on the last album [*1984*]. Some of the other titles were "Babe Don't Leave Me Alone" and "Peace of Mind." Good tunes, but, Van Halen-wise, kind of dated. They're a little dumber rock.

GW: Whose idea was it to use Sunset Sound, the studio where the first albums were recorded?

VAN HALEN: Donn and Ted had basically done all the Doobie Brothers stuff there; it was one of their favorite places. I didn't know anything about studios, so wherever they wanted to go was okay.

GW: What was the first song you recorded?

VAN HALEN: I don't remember. "On Fire," I think. I played the harmonics at the beginning on the A and D strings, one fret down from the E position [*seventh fret*] on the A string. It's actually not a harmonic; it's just a muffled, dead, weird sound. It sounded kind of machine-like. We wanted a little break between verses, and I said, "This is neat, how about this? It sounds rude."

GW: Did you use a sitar on "Ain't Talkin' 'Bout Love"?

VAN HALEN: I doubled that one part. It could have been a Coral guitar, but it looked real cheap. It looked like a Danelectro with some kind of stuff muffling the strings back there. I never really knew it was an electric sitar, because it didn't sound like one. It just sounded like a buzzy-fretted guitar. The thing was real bizarre.

GW: How did you get that swishing sound on the intro to "Atomic Punk"?

VAN HALEN: I used an MXR Phase 90 and rubbed my palm over the pickup. And then during two of the breaks I used an MXR flanger.

GW: You used MXR pedals from the beginning?

VAN HALEN: Yeah. I don't really use them anymore. I just use an Echoplex.

GW: The guitar shown on the cover of the first album is the one you built?

VAN HALEN: It's the same guitar I used on all the albums, and all the tours up until the *1984* tour. It was my baby until I started using the Kramers. For a while I was putting Kramer necks on that main guitar [*pictured on the* Van Halen *cover*]. For the second album [Van Halen II], I had that black and yellow guitar [*pictured on the back cover*].

GW: Why did you change your guitar?

VAN HALEN: I don't know why I played that black and yellow one. I liked the way it looked, but I didn't like the way it sounded. Actually, I used an Ibanez Destroyer for a lot of *Van Halen*—the guitar that is on the *Women and Children First* cover. On all the stuff that didn't have any vibrato on it, I used the Ibanez. "You Really Got Me," the rhythm track of "Jamie's Cryin' " and "On Fire," too. It has a PAF on it. It was one of the few guitars made out of Korina wood that you could get, without spending an arm and a leg for an original "V" or something. It was a great-sounding guitar—until I took a chunk out of it to make it look nice, to make it look different. On the cover of *Women and Children First*, it's missing a piece. Boy, did I screw it up.

GW: It changed the sound?

VAN HALEN: Oh, completely. It ruined it. [*laughs*] It went from sounding like a nice, fat, warm guitar to, "What the hell happened?" I couldn't believe it. The sound changed from a fat, Les Paul-type sound to a real weak Strat sound. I thought I'd ruined the pickup when I took the chunk of wood out, so I stuck in another pickup. But it sounded the same—real bad. I think it was because I took the wood out right by the bridge; that's where a lot of resonance and tone come from.

GW: What is that story about Angel almost releasing "You Really Got Me" before Van Halen did?

VAN HALEN: Yeah. A couple of guys from Angel were friends, acquaintances. One day—I forget where we were, it might have been the Rainbow—I was braggin' about our album, saying, "Hey, this is bad, you ought to listen to this." Because they had been talking about their new stuff. So we went up to [*drummer*] Barry Brandt's house, and they were all blown away by the album. They were all listening very carefully to this and that, and I left there feeling real good and proud. The next morning Ted Templeman called me up and said, "Did you play that tape for anybody?" And I said, "Yeah, I played it for all kinds of people!" He was pissed. I didn't know, nobody told me not to play it for anyone. I guess they figured I knew. And he said, "You asshole, why did you do that?" Because through the grapevine, Ted heard that Angel went into the studio and was trying to put out a single of "You Really Got Me" before us.

GW: That really wouldn't have changed anything...

VAN HALEN: I think it could have hurt. [*laughs*] So we released it as soon as possible—even before the album was out, I think. We had performed that song live for years. When we recorded demo tapes with Ted and Donn, that was actually the last song we did. Ted said then, "Well, you got anything else?" And we said, "Well, we've got some cover tunes." He said, "Play 'em."

It kind of bummed me out that Ted wanted our first single to be someone else's tune. I would have maybe picked "Jamie's Cryin'," just because it was our own.

GW: Did the success of "You Really Got Me" lead to your doing another cover for the second album?

VAN HALEN: I don't know how "You're No Good" came about. I guess it was Ted. He figured, "Hey, it worked the first time, let's try it again." I really don't remember how it ended up being picked. I didn't even remember how the damn song went. We used to play it in the bars, at Gazarri's, but we didn't play it like that. We played it like the original [*Linda Ronstadt*] record. I know how this version came about, but I don't know how it came about that we used the song. Ted hummed the tune to me, and that's how I came up with the riff; I was just trying to noodle my way through it to figure out the chords. We never listened to the record to learn it. So I don't know if it's right or not.

GW: Was "Spanish Fly" designed to follow-up "Eruption"?

VAN HALEN: Al and I spent New Year's Eve, 1979, over at Ted Templeman's house. He had an acoustic guitar sitting in a corner, and I picked it up. I was getting drunk—and started playing it. I remember Ted saying, "Wow!" You can play acoustic guitar too?" And I said, "Yeah, I guess. It has six strings. It's not really any different." And I started doing hammer-ons—whoever came up with that name, hammer-ons?—and I started doing that stuff on the fingerboard and Ted said, "Hey, why don't you do something for the next record on acoustic guitar?" And I said, "Okay, sure." I bought a nylon-string Ovation and used it for that, and I don't know what happened to it. It took two or three takes.

GW: Do you remember when hammer-ons became part of your style?

VAN HALEN: I think it was around the end of the Gazarri's days.

GW: Had you heard of anyone playing like that?

VAN HALEN: Honestly, no. I'm sure people had but I'd never seen anyone.

GW: The sound of the bass on the first two albums seemed to be a little buried.

VAN HALEN: I guess the sound Mike was getting at the time was either smothering everything if it was too loud or impossible to hear if you put it where it fit.

GW: Did you suggest bass parts?

VAN HALEN: Some things would just obviously follow the guitar-type of stuff, unless I had a specific bass line. Otherwise, Mike does whatever he feels like doing.

GW: Moving on to *Women and Children First*, did the album mark the first time you used a keyboard in the studio?

VAN HALEN: Yeah, on "And the Cradle Will Rock." I had an old Wurlitzer electric piano and I pumped it through my Marshalls. A lot of people don't even know that because it doesn't really sound like a keyboard. That was my first encounter with the band not wanting me to play keyboards—when we did the song live, Mike played it. They didn't want a "guitar hero" playing keyboards, and that kind of ties in with why they didn't want "Jump."

GW: Did you think about staging a keyboard-oriented song?

VAN HALEN: Yeah. I saw no harm in my playing keyboards, as long as I do it well. I still think I should have played "And the Cradle Will Rock" live because Mike is not as much of a keyboard player as I am. He can be taught, like anybody can, but since I played it on the record and wrote it, I figured I could play it a little better.

GW: Did you put an effect on the Wurlitzer for the record?

VAN HALEN: I just banged on the lower part of the keyboard—no notes, just a cluster—and switched on my MXR flanger.

GW: The break in "Romeo Delight" had a real Who-type feel to it. Were you aiming for a *Live at Leeds* quality?

VAN HALEN: It just kind of happened. I never try to get a certain kind of feeling. I just try to get any type of feeling at all—whatever comes out. [*laughs*] Whatever came out is the feeling I got.

GW: There's also a heartbeat sound on "Romeo Delight."

VAN HALEN: I think Mike was picking quietly, and I tapped my string against the pickup poles.

GW: Was that the Stratocaster?

VAN HALEN: I think that was the Ibanez. I butchered it for the photo session after the record was recorded.

   [*Sometime after this conversation took place, Edward remembered borrowing an Ibanez Destroyer from Chris Holmes of W.A.S.P. and using it for portions of the* Women and Children First *album.—GW Ed.*]

GW: At the beginning of "Fools," you play some Eric Clapton-style blues.

VAN HALEN: Yeah; I don't know where that came from. I think it was

Ted's idea to get Dave's voice to sound that way. He wanted people to hear a different side of Dave's voice. That backup kind of blues guitar seemed to fit. That was the Ibanez.

GW: There are all kinds of effects happening in the intro of "Everybody Wants Some!!"

VAN HALEN: I did kind of a cello thing on the low E string with the palm of my hand. It's the same technique used on "Atomic Punk," but I'm not hitting all the strings.

GW: Did you double the rhythm part to get that fat sound on "Everybody Wants Some!!"?

VAN HALEN: No, I've never doubled a rhythm part. I don't know, I just turn it up, I guess. Everything is on 10. We just use cheap Shure 57s.

GW: What is the effect on the guitar on "Tora! Tora!"?

VAN HALEN: That's backwards, and we kicked an Echo Plate [EMT] at the end of it. Just for fun.

GW: What kind of acoustic guitar do you play on "Take Your Whisky Home"?

VAN HALEN: I don't know what that was; just a rented job.

GW: Do you enjoy playing acoustic guitar?

VAN HALEN: Not really. It's not loud enough.

GW: Isn't there also an acoustic on "Could This Be Magic?"

VAN HALEN: Yeah, and I played slide on that for the first time in my life. It was kind of funny. Dave and I played together, and I don't know, I guess we had a little difference in rhythm. Like on "Ice Cream Man," Dave played the guitar, that little acoustic part. I just used some glass job for the slide. I had listened to Duane Allman a little bit on *Layla*, but slide is something that has never really interested me. I played in standard tuning.

GW: What is that little piece of music that just fades into nothingness at the very end of side two?

VAN HALEN: It was something Al and I were working on. I forget what we called it—"Growth," or something like that. We thought that just for the hell of it we'd stick it at the end of the record. And possibly start the next record with it. But it never amounted to anything, so we left it at that.

GW: To my mind, *Fair Warning* took Van Halen to a higher level in terms of record production. There were more guitar parts and more textures. Is that accurate?

VAN HALEN: I guess. I remember I approached my playing a little differently, where almost every song had an overdub in it, whereas before it was kept way down to a minimum. I wrote rhythm parts that I intended to solo over.

GW: Are you able to hear in your head what the various parts will sound like when they're finally put together?

VAN HALEN: Yeah, I usually can tell, but sometimes what I hear in my head doesn't work. But the majority of the time it does.

GW: You did some of the writing for *Fair Warning* on piano?

VAN HALEN: I did some stuff on piano and some stuff that still hasn't been used—obviously. [*laughs*] The album took a long time to record, because I was getting married and this and that. In the same way *1984* took the longest because the US Festival got in the way. We'd start to record, and then we'd have to make a radio program, etc. Every time we'd start to record it was [*in nasal voice*], "Oh, yeah, we forgot to tell you, you owe us this by tomorrow." The US Festival was actually like a whole tour's worth of work for one hour of playing—everything from the stage set-up to rehearsing for it to all the video stuff that we owed them. I know Donn and I were happy to wash our hands clean of that when it was done.

GW: It didn't seem to mar the success of *1984* at all.

VAN HALEN: No, it didn't. But if we would have had to have the record out at a certain deadline in the middle of that, it would have suffered. But we said, "Screw 'em. We'll put it out when it's damn well ready."

GW: What is the technique you use at the beginning of "Mean Streets"?

VAN HALEN: I tapped on the 12th fret of the low E and the 12th fret of the high E, and muffled both with my left hand down by the nut. I got kind of a funk slap out of the guitar. I applied to guitar what bass players do when they slap. But it's not like I studied it or anything.

GW: The solo on "Mean Streets" was very aggressive. Were you an angry young man that day?

VAN HALEN: [*laughs*] I wasn't trying to be mad, but it just seemed to fit. I think I did do some interesting solos on the *Fair Warning* album.

GW: You decided to try your hand at slide again on "Dirty Movies."

VAN HALEN: I came up with the melody of it on slide, so I played it on the record on slide. The funny thing was I couldn't get up high enough on the guitar, so I sawed part of it off. I used an old Les Paul Junior that had an SG body style and that one hook...what do you call it?

GW: Horn?

VAN HALEN: Horn. Yeah, the bottom one was in the way, so I took a hacksaw right there in the studio and said, "Hold this, Ted," and sawed it off.

GW: The bass sound on *Fair Warning* was much better than it was on the previous records.

VAN HALEN: Yeah. We used different amps, smaller amps—smaller amps usually get a better bass sound.

GW: Didn't you do something interesting with the solo in "So This is Love"?

VAN HALEN: Out of six solo tracks, Ted let me mess around a little bit, but I don't think he thought I could get anything. Then Donn showed up and said, "Why don't you try it once?" I thought I was just trying it, but he recorded my composite and that was my first attempt. It's like four solos punched together. That surprised a few people.

GW: Do you go through different feels for a solo before coming up with one that you think will work?

VAN HALEN: I don't know. It's not an intentional, planned-out thing. Whatever sounds right, I guess.

GW: Do you know if it's right when you hear it back?

VAN HALEN: Yeah. Obviously, you'd better know if it's right when you hear it back. If not, you're up the creek.

GW: "Sunday Afternoon in the Park" was another song that featured synthesizer.

VAN HALEN: It was one of those cheap little kid's toys, an Electro Harmonix. It didn't have any notes; you could rub your hand across the whole octave of the board and it would go *rrrrrrrrrrrrrr* [*rolls tongue and imitates sequencer line*]. I just blazed it through the Marshalls. It was cheaper than a Casio, and was made of cardboard, plastic and a little sensor keyboard.

GW: Could this have been the seed for "Jump"?

VAN HALEN: As a matter of fact, I might have had "Jump" by then.

GW: You approached the tracks on *Diver Down* differently than you did those of the first four albums.

VAN HALEN: Basically, we did more finishing up of individual tracks before moving on to the next.

GW: You did four cover songs on *Diver Down*.

VAN HALEN: That was too many—four too many. Dave always wanted to redo "Dancing in the Streets," and I remember him giving me a tape of it. I said, "I can't get a handle on anything out of this." I didn't want to do it, I didn't like it. So I suggested "Pretty Woman," because that seemed more a Van Halen song to cover. It was us. I was working on something on the Mini-Moog, and Ted happened to hear the riff and said, "Wow, we can use this for "Dancing in the Streets." So Ted and Dave were happy—and I wasn't. Because the riff I had for something else got used for a song I didn't even want to do.

GW: You used a Moog for that song?

VAN HALEN: A MiniMoog with a delay set so it would go [*sings rhythm of song*]. It wasn't a sequencer; I've never used a sequencer.

GW: Have you studied the workings of synthesizers to learn what they can really do?

VAN HALEN: Only sound-wise. Not to the extent of most people. I don't know crap about 'em, really. I can play keyboards, and I twist the knobs until I get the sound that I like.

GW: Did guitar synthesizer ever interest you?

VAN HALEN: No. For many people it's a good instrument because they play guitar and don't play keyboards. But I figure, if you play keyboards, why bother having to change the way you play guitar in order to adapt to that? I prefer playing keyboards if I'm going to play synthesizer.

GW: Were you using the Kramers for this record?

VAN HALEN: I've never used a Kramer on record. I only got them for the *1984* tour. I may have put a Kramer neck on the guitars.

GW: What attracts you to the Kramer?

VAN HALEN: I just like their guitars. I play one all the time now, for recording and everything. The stuff I did for *The Wild Life* film was all on the Kramer.

GW: You used a Fender Stratocaster on "Cathedral."

VAN HALEN: Yeah, with an echo setting similar to that of "Dancing in the Streets," except it was a little slower so you could get that arpeggiated sound.

GW: And you played a 12-string on "Secrets"?

VAN HALEN: Yeah, one of those Gibson double-neck jobs. They were too heavy. I played it live and my shoulder was aching afterwards. No wonder Jimmy Page has a slouch.

GW: How did people react to "Secrets"?

VAN HALEN: I thought it was a great song. It was different for us. Not for the sake of being different, but since we have something different we might as well stick it out there. I think that should have been the single before "Dancing in the Streets." But somehow it just got lost in the shuffle.

GW: What guitar did you use on "Little Guitars"?

VAN HALEN: We were on tour in Memphis during *Fair Warning*, and sitting on the steps outside the hotel was a kid named David Petschulat, who stopped me and said, "Here, Eddie, check this out." And I went, "Wow." It was a perfect replica of an older Les Paul, except it was one third the size. I tripped, it was neat. So I took it to sound check and plugged it in. It sounded like a normal guitar, except higher in pitch. I started playing around on it and came up with the music for "Little Guitars." Later on, Billy Gibbons gave me a couple of those little Chiquita jobs, but I never really played them.

GW: Which brings us to the *1984* album. If *Van Halen, Van Halen II* and *Women and Children First* represent the first phase of the band's development, and *Fair Warning* and *Diver Down* represent the second level, then *1984* surely must be the third phase?

VAN HALEN: In a way, it's Phase One of Donn and Ed. Donn and I were very involved in this record. We almost took control, to a point, because it was done here in our studio, and we knew what we wanted. We weren't about to let the album be puked out in any way—especially since it was done here. We wanted it to be an accurate representation of the sound of this studio, and in a way I guess we were proving ourselves—to ourselves, more than anybody. I think everything sounds the best; I like it all.

GW: Did you play any other guitars besides the Stratocaster?

VAN HALEN: I used a Gibson Flying V on "Hot for Teacher" and "Drop Dead Legs." Actually, I've used a lot of different guitars, recording-wise, but live I usually use just one. I used the V because I needed the pickup switch to do the quiet part in "Hot for Teacher." Live, I used a Roland echo box with a volume knob on it, and I hooked it up to my pedal boards so I could hit the pedal and drop the volume, because I couldn't reach for the knob quick enough on the guitar. That song was beyond any boogie I've ever heard. It was pretty powerful.

GW: *1984* was the first album in which you used the Ripley stereo guitar [*an instrument built by Steve Ripley in which each string can be sent to different sides of the speakers through the use of individual string pan pots—GW Ed.*].

VAN HALEN: I used that on "Top Jimmy." It's not really a stereo guitar; it has an individual pan pot for each string, so you can designate where each note you're playing will come out in the stereo spectrum. And I panned each string opposite each other, so the low E string would come out way left and the A string would come out right in the stereo picture. We used it on another thing, called "Ripley," that we didn't use on the record. It's a great guitar—a different guitar. You need two amps for it. There's another one that has built-in vibrato, and is actually like a miniature console with send and receive effects, and a patch bay where you can put a different effect on each string. I haven't gotten into that, but I can just imagine having a different effect on each string, panning it wherever you want, and adding vibrato to it. It's basically a guitar for the Eighties—or Nineties.

GW: Weren't you toying around with the idea of building your own amplifier for production?

VAN HALEN: Jose Aredondo, who works on my amps, and I had some ideas of building our own and selling it as my amp. It'll definitely be an amp that sounds the way I want it to. It will have everything you could possibly want in an amp for good sound.

GW: Getting back to the *1984* album, what keyboard did you use for "Jump"?

VAN HALEN: I used an OBX-A. They stopped making them, so now I play an OB-8, which is a better keyboard. You can basically get the same sounds out of it; there's just a slight difference between the two. To my ears, the OBX-A seems to have a little warmer sound, but the OB-8 is much more dependable.

GW: So you were fiddling around in the studio—hearing a sound and thinking that it would be right for the song?

VAN HALEN: Yeah. I just knew what sound I wanted to noodle with; not necessarily for "Jump," but just to noodle with. Whenever I sit down, I know what kind of sound I'm looking for.

GW: You've described your guitar sound as the "brown" sound. What color is your keyboard sound?

VAN HALEN: The same. Brown. I play brown to drums, everything. It's just a warm sound. Warm, big, majestic.

GW: Did you wonder what guitar fans would think about your playing keyboard?

VAN HALEN: No; I think the band wondered about it. I think as long as you do something well, what's the difference? I just knew that everyone from my father to the guy who works on my cars loved it. It had a universal appeal to it. If people didn't like it, that's fine, too. I knew what it was. Donn and I liked it so much, we didn't care what anybody else thought about it, I guess.

GW: Were there many takes before the final version?

VAN HALEN: I think we just did it once. Actually, the tape ran out at the very end, just in time. That's why we had to be careful with the fade at the end. When Donn mixed it, he had to fade it just right; otherwise he would have run out of tape.

GW: Did you play the keyboard on the basic track?

VAN HALEN: Yeah, we were all out there at the same time, and then I put the guitar on. The guitar at the end of the song was actually another song. We laid down that other track, too. Also, we were going to redo "In the Midnight Hour," but ended up not using it. The solo in "Jump" was spontaneous; I don't know if it was a first take.

GW: Your main contribution to the *1984* album was as keyboardist. Any thoughts on that?

VAN HALEN: No. [*laughs*] It's neat. It's almost like I play more keyboards now than I do guitar. I enjoy playing keyboards. It means you don't have to jump around on stage and have something hanging round your neck. No, I'm joking.

GW: Did the overall success of *1984* give the band more freedom to wander outside the boundaries?

VAN HALEN: It gave me the freedom to play keyboards comfortably. Now I don't have to worry about what the rest of the guys think other people will think. I never worried about what anyone thinks, except it makes you feel kind of uncertain when the guys worry.

GW: Did you think about staging "Jump" live?

VAN HALEN: No. I just figured I'd cut the solo out because it's such a short little thing, or play it on keyboard, which I did. Mike played a MiniMoog bass live, since I did some counter-melodies on the record that I didn't have enough hands for.

GW: "I'll Wait" was another keyboard song.

VAN HALEN: That was one they really didn't want. It was actually that, more than "Jump," they didn't want to touch with a 10-foot pole. So Donn and I basically did the track with Al. Ted and Dave didn't like it.

GW: Where did the song "1984" come from?

VAN HALEN: The intro? That was the very first thing we ever did in this studio here. I was out there noodling on a synthesizer, and Donn was recording it without my knowledge. It was 45 minutes of me noodling like that. And we ended up using part of it.

GW: Having 5150 must have opened up a new world for you.

VAN HALEN: Oh, yeah. *1984* would not have been what it is if it wasn't done here.

GW: What about some of the non-Van Halen projects with which you've been involved, like writing the music for *The Wild Life*?

VAN HALEN: Donn and I saw the script for *The Wild Life* and said we'd do something for it. We ended up doing just about the whole film. It was fun, but we were kind of under pressure because of the deadlines. I had to leave to go on tour again, so I sort of left Donn to finish the mixing and everything. I played all the instruments.

GW: How come there is only one song ["Donut City"] on the soundtrack album?

VAN HALEN: We didn't really want anything on it. The songs on the record aren't even in the movie. We said that if they had to have something on the album, take "Donut City." We were concerned about doing stuff for the film, not selling a record.

GW: And you did some music for Valerie's [*Bertinelli, Eddie's wife*] film, *The Seduction of Gina*?

VAN HALEN: Yeah, two songs. That was fun. Film music is much different than making an album. You sit there, watch the screen and think what would work.

GW: What about the Brian May & Friends [*Star Fleet Project*] album?

VAN HALEN: That was just a get-together jam. He invited me down to the Record Plant and we played. I didn't know he was planning to do a record. After we played, he called me up about four months later and asked what I thought about putting the stuff out. And I said, "Send me a tape, let me hear it first," because I didn't remember how it went. He did and I said, "Sure, what the hell." It reeks of fun. I broke a string in one of the blues jams and we just kept going; we didn't fix it. Brian is good. He gets a brown sound.

GW: And you played on a Nicolette Larson album [*Nicolette*]?

VAN HALEN: Yeah, I played on one song. That was a favor for Ted.

GW: Have you worked a long time at developing the "brown sound"?

VAN HALEN: Not really. Yes and no. It's basically a tone, a feeling that I'm always working at. Everything is involved in that, and I've been working with it since I've been playing. It comes from the person.

GW: Was the brown sound being developed when you were listening to Eric Clapton and learning all his solos?

VAN HALEN: I don't know. It was always the live stuff I was into.

GW: Could you listen to "Crossroads," for example, and pick out the solo note-for-note?

VAN HALEN: Not that easily. Because the way Baker, Bruce and Clapton played live, those guys twisted and bent to the ultimate extremes of 4/4. There was something about them that I say about myself, though I'm not saying I'm in their league or bitchin' in that way at all, but they had a quality of falling down the stairs and landing on their feet. Listen to "I'm So Glad," on *Goodbye Cream*. Incredible, man! For my mind, nothing has matched it to this day. It was totally reckless-abandon-but-knowing-where-you're-goin'. People used to think I was nuts to sit there and listen over and over to what they would call noise. I don't even care if they knew what the other guy was doing. Going from total confusion to clicking together blew me away. I'm sure they weren't that good every night.

GW: That's the key.

VAN HALEN: Exactly. In a fun way, pushing yourself for yourself. Pushing yourself to a limit and taking a chance.

GW: Does Van Halen take chances?

VAN HALEN: Al and I do, all the time. Dave doesn't really like it and Mike isn't really plugged in with Al and me, so he kind of stops and lets us go crazy. Al and I just jam; sometimes we get carried away and go for too long, and we'll hear about it after the show. The next night we'll do it even longer! I'm joking. We don't do it on purpose; we do it because, to me, that's what making music is about. And that's what I always loved about Cream. They made music exciting in a way I don't think people really understood. It was almost as if the lyric and actual song structure was secondary. "Let's get this shit over with so we can make music and see where we land tonight." I loved that.

GW: Have you done that on record?

VAN HALEN: No. We've captured feelings to that effect but we've never put anything on record that is a jam, where somebody starts something, somebody follows and you work off each other. Al and I do that all the time by ourselves, but we've never put that on record because it's not a hit single. But who cares about a hit single?

GW: Maybe that's where an album on your own might come in.

VAN HALEN: Oh yeah, sure. But why even bother? Why not just do it and feel good about having done it?

GW: You said earlier you weren't interested in hit singles. It seems you're sure that if you find enjoyment in it, other people wouldn't. That's not necessarily the case.

VAN HALEN: That's true. But I guess I don't understand the rationale for putting something that personal out. And I guess Cream had more balls than I ever had. They did that, and said, "Here we are." I guess the closest we've gotten to that is the first album, which was basically recorded live in the studio.

GW: And that first album really captured a moment.

VAN HALEN: It was different. But if the next album had been the same, then it wouldn't have been different, would it? It's very difficult to figure out what to do on record. Maybe that's why I haven't done one on my own. I'm partly brainwashed by the whole aspect of the business—that there's something expected of me. What if I did something totally off the wall that I personally enjoyed, and people thought something weird about me? In a way, I guess, it's exposing a side of yourself that is very difficult to expect anyone to understand in the slightest way. I'd rather not even expose myself or that type of music to any attack. You know how sometimes you can do something just for fun and people take it like it's your statement? I guess I don't even want anything to do with that whole thing. Do you understand?

GW: To me, "Jump" was taking a chance—a keyboard tune from the guitarist of the Eighties.

VAN HALEN: "Jump" was not a spontaneous jam. What I was talking about was that live-Cream, spontaneous thing. For one, it would take somebody with a hell of a sense of humor, and they'd have to be a musician to even get anything out of it. I'm talking total darkness concerning format—no form, no song structure, nothing. Maybe someday... At the moment, I'm just writing. We're talking about doing another Van Halen album.

GW: A live recording?

VAN HALEN: No, I don't see the purpose.

GW: What do you do when you're not in the studio?

VAN HALEN: Sleep.

GW: Would you like to have a family?

VAN HALEN: Yeah, I'd love to have a family, but it's not really the right time in my life. Maybe within a year or two.

GW: Would you want your child to be a musician?

VAN HALEN: Sure, why not? Only if he wants to be; I wouldn't force him. I think he or she will be exposed to music in an unforced way, and it will be their own choice. Of course, I'll try exposing them to it.

GW: You told me once that most of the music you hear on the radio sounds the same.

VAN HALEN: Well, doesn't it? There's such a handful of heavy metal bands, that God, I can't tell the difference. There's no unique quality that sticks out in my ear. They all play as fast as they can, as loud as they can, scream as high as they can, but they don't even scream, or play fast, with a unique quality. They don't.

GW: You also said some players do have good guitar sounds, but something is missing.

VAN HALEN: Yeah. I don't know what it is. It leaves me cold. Obviously it doesn't leave everyone cold, because they sell records like hell. The state of rock and roll right now is like incest. You have bands that are clones, and you have bands who are clones of clones— and they all start copying each other to the point where it's like incest. And obviously you're going to have retarded kids. [*laughs*]

GW: I asked you earlier if you wanted to be Beethoven. What about being a guitarist during the Sixties, playing alongside musicians like Page and Clapton?

VAN HALEN: Yeah, I guess. It would have been fun.

GW: If the moment had never arrived for you, would you be content still playing Gazarri's?

VAN HALEN: Yeah. I love making music just for the sake of doing it. My dad is starting to teach me how to play saxophone. I'd really like to get into that; I love saxophone. But it's tough, it's a hard instrument. For me it is, anyway. And I'm going to go out and buy a cello, too.

GW: So for your solo record we can expect to hear a...

VAN HALEN: A synthesizer-saxophone-cello-piano album. [*laughs*] We'll call it *Guitar? What Guitar?*

GW: I just have a feeling that when we next hear Van Halen they won't be...

VAN HALEN: The same? Maybe you're right. I guess we'll all have to sit around and wait, and see what that difference will be. I don't really know. It's definitely time to move on.

GUITAR WORLD, SEPTEMBER 1986

ON THE ROAD

David Lee Roth was out, Sammy Hagar was in, and GUITAR WORLD was there with the inside scoop.
By Steven Rosen

G **UITAR WORLD:** You seem so happy with the new band.

EDWARD VAN HALEN: Dave always said I'm not happy unless I'm unhappy, so to speak. And that's a crock—I'm happy as hell and I'm coming up with some great stuff.

GW: Will you ever look back at those years with Dave and regret that it all fell apart?

VAN HALEN: Hell no. It was a blessing in disguise. When we get nominated for a Grammy and win, I'm going to thank him. [*laughs*] I'm serious.

GW: Have you heard any of the music Dave's been working on?

VAN HALEN: I hear it's good. [*Bassist*] Billy Sheehan is a bad mother—one of the best around.

GW: They may have songwriting problems—Dave doesn't write, and Steve Vai doesn't write those types of songs.

VAN HALEN: And Billy writes heavy metal riffs.

GW: So he'll have to find outside writers.

VAN HALEN: He already bought some tunes from Steve Lukather. Steve is such a nice guy, he actually asked me, "Hey, do you mind?" I said, "Hell no, I don't mind." Billy Sheehan kind of asked me the same thing. And I said, "What do you think? Dave just left the band

and he wants the hottest guns in town to replace us." And he asked, "Well, hey, we're still friends, right?" And I said, "Sure, I don't care. I got no beef with you." Actually, I've got no beef with Dave either— it's just that he really hurt me. You know? That's what it boils down to, and that's why I was so pissed off in the very beginning. At the height of our career—you work at something for so long, and all of a sudden someone just pulls the plug on you. That's kind of cruel.

GW: Did Dave really pull the plug?

VAN HALEN: Yeah, he quit! We weren't getting along, but we never did, basically.

GW: Didn't you want to leave the band several years ago?

VAN HALEN: Yeah, four years ago. During *Fair Warning*. I wanted to quit, but I stuck with it, and that's what burns my ass even more. If I would have quit then I wouldn't have spent an extra four years putting up with his attitude. I mean, hey, the guy's creative, okay? But he's a lousy human. Trying to live with the guy on tour… You ask anybody that's gone on tour with us, and they'll tell you he'd yell and scream for his apple in the morning. Or ransack people's rooms for the *Playboy* somebody borrowed the night before.

GW: Power trips?

VAN HALEN: Oh yeah. And Noel Monk [*the band's manager at the time*] was his goddamn puppet—did everything he wanted. And that's partly why Al and I wanted to change; we wanted a manager who managed the band—not someone who did only what one person said.

GW: Had you left during *Fair Warning*, it would have been…

VAN HALEN: Different, sure. Well, let's put it this way: The end result is, I'm very happy now. Whatever it took to get where I am now, I'm very happy.

GW: Was "Dreams," from the new album, played on the MIDIed piano?

VAN HALEN: Yeah, I think so. We never even got to work with Dave on that; we rehearsed maybe for a total of a week within a month's time.

GW: So he had heard some of the new material?

VAN HALEN: Oh, yeah, I had "Good Enough" and "Summer Nights," and we'd begun work on "Dreams."

GW: It appears from *5150* that your writing has moved in new directions.

VAN HALEN: It's constantly changing, I guess. I don't really know where inspiration comes from—or where anything comes from.

GW: Was there any worry about the ideas not being there?

VAN HALEN: Oh, not at all. The way I feel about it is, Sammy and I are in tune with each other. I have to say that, often, opposites will attract. Dave and I were completely opposite in our backgrounds and music, our musical styles and what we enjoyed listening to. And sometimes that works. The friction creates something.

GW: Like with the Who?

VAN HALEN: Yeah, but there Pete Townshend writes everything. With Sammy, we're the same—and it seems to work better. So the theory that opposites attract is not valid in this case.

GW: Did you listen to many singers before finding Sammy? I know you listened to [*Australian vocalist*] Jimmy Barnes.

VAN HALEN: And he's doing well. I got a tape from him, and it's the same record he has out now. I don't know; he's a great singer, but I didn't think he was right for the type of music that I write.

GW: Did you think that having Hagar in the band would make it sound like Sammy Hagar's band? As opposed to some unknown vocalist?

VAN HALEN: I think Sammy Hagar's work on this record is like nothing he's ever done. No, I never thought we would sound like Sammy Hagar, because I'd be writing the music, and my music doesn't sound like Sammy Hagar music. I pulled some vocals out of him where even Sammy kind of flipped and said, "Whoa, I didn't know I could do that." I guess we pushed each other.

GW: Was Mick Jones important in that area?

VAN HALEN: I produced all the vocals with Sammy except for "Dreams," because Mick was on tour. Mick helped out a great deal in organizing things. You know how I am—"Hey, let's work on this today. Nah, let's work on that." Or whatever. He really helped pull it all together and polish it up, so to speak. Mick changed a few things and he offered a few ideas. He and I wrote "Dreams" with Sammy. The song was completely different than it is now. Originally, what is now the verse part was actually a part of the solo section. The same parts were still there but they were juggled around. And he tore a hell of a vocal out of Sammy on that one. Mick is great to work with, a nice guy. We call him "The Duke." A proper English guy.

GW: How did you meet him?

VAN HALEN: I met him through Sammy at the MTV Awards. Now, it's in our contract that Warner Bros. has the right to refuse producers. I wanted the band to do it by ourselves with Donn, and they said, "No." So what we did was, we went ahead and did the whole record anyway, and then brought Mick in and had him kind of oversee it. But I think Warner knows now that I'm not the flake that I've been reputed to be.

GW: Billy Gibbons had a similar experience—no one was sure about the idea of bringing synthesizers into ZZ Top, and he just asked for a chance to be heard. I think they believe him now.

VAN HALEN: Yeah. [*Warner Bros. production executive*] Lenny Waronker was a great help. He came down and heard stuff that we were doing, and he was flattened—floored. He said, "Whoa, I didn't think you guys could pull it off." After he heard a couple of cuts he said, "Go for it," even before Mick showed up. Then he began to trust us.

GW: How come you're not working with Ted Templeman anymore?

VAN HALEN: Actually, he came to one rehearsal. We showed him about four or five tunes. He made notes and everything, but he had a commitment to Dave. He didn't know when he was going to be working with Dave, and it just so happened that we wanted to start—we wanted to get rolling. I got sick of sitting on my ass. It's funny that Dave says we wanted to sit on our butts and stay at home and not tour and not work. I sat on my thumbs waiting for him for eight months, and I didn't want to wait another month to start recording. And Ted said, "I have a previous commitment," and we said, "Okay, fine, see ya later." It wasn't like we split. I'm not saying we'll never work with him again; it wasn't that type of thing. Ted is great, but he took Dave's side. But it was obviously because he committed himself to Dave after his *Crazy from the Heat* thing.

GW: Perhaps Ted has more control over Dave than he does over you.

VAN HALEN: Oh, sure, yeah. With us he'd have to put up with me. [*laughs*] Which I don't know if he's into too much.

GW: Logistically, then, if Ted could have produced both the Roth and Van Halen albums, you would have agreed to that?

VAN HALEN: [*pauses*] Probably, yeah...I don't know, it's hard to say. Put it this way, he was our number one choice because, obviously, he knows me and Alex and Mike and Sammy very well [*Templeman produced Hagar's* VOA *album and the Montrose records.—GW Ed.*]. And he and Donn have worked together for years. So it just seemed like a logical thing. Whatever differences there may have been, it could have worked. At least from my end.

GW: I get the impression that you wanted to be more involved in *5150*.

VAN HALEN: Oh, sure. The way we did this record is basically how I would like to have done all the previous ones. And I think that's another thing that maybe drove Dave away. For *1984*, I built the studio, and began wanting to do things a little more my way. I guess I turned some people off; I created a little friction, though unintentionally. I built the studio for the benefit of all of us, for the family, for the band. But I guess certain people didn't look at it that way, because Ted sure didn't dig working up there. Even though he loves the sound of the place, he just kind of looked at it like if I got pissed at him, I'd kick him out of my studio. [*laughs*] Though I'd never do that. If anything, Dave is the one who did that.

GW: Do you wish you could've worked with Dave the same way you do with Sammy?

VAN HALEN: I don't know. I don't know if I could have gotten out of Dave what I can get out of Sammy. I don't know if this is slandering Dave, but Sammy is just a better singer; he can do anything I ask him to do. Whereas Ted has a much better handle on what to get out of Dave, because Dave is kind of limited, vocally—range-wise and stuff. I don't know if that's a bad thing to say. I don't know how that is going to look in print. But I mean, hey, Dave has a unique voice and a unique style and also has a very strong idea of what he wants. So does Sammy, but I just pushed him a little further. Gave him a little confidence and said, "Hey, hit this note." And he'd go even higher than the note I asked him to hit. He'd be blown away and it would be great.

GW: Did the fact that Sammy had greater facility than Dave lead to a change in your approach to writing songs?

VAN HALEN: Sure. Like in "Why Can't This Be Love?" there is this part [*sings the middle part where the voice doubles the keyboard*]. I would never have attempted to ask Dave to do that.

GW: The *5150* sessions felt good with Sammy?

VAN HALEN: More than anything. He's changed my life. Seriously. He bought a house two doors away from me and we get along great. It's like we've known each other all our lives, really. Very close.

GW: Why wouldn't Dave allow himself to be a friend?

VAN HALEN: I don't know. Well, in the beginning I guess we were, kind of. But he was always too much into being a star. And that is what he is. I'm a musician, he's a star. A musician doesn't want to go and star, direct and write his own movie. We were really just different people. Sammy and I are a little more the same. A little more human, so to speak. [*laughs*]

GW: Is the feeling in the band now similar to what you experienced during the very early days of Van Halen?

VAN HALEN: Dave pretty much always had that edge to him—that attitude. I don't know where it came from—insecurity, or having to prove something to his peers. But he always had that uncomfortable kind of attitude of never letting his guard down and opening up and actually letting you inside him. Sometimes I wouldn't know what kind of mood he was in. He's so moody sometimes that you only converse when he wants to. Whatever. Not much more about him, okay?

GW: Okay. Getting back to the music, did you really meet Sammy through Claudio [*Edward's and Sammy's mechanic, who is pictured at the outset of Hagar's "I Can't Drive 55" video*]?

VAN HALEN: Yes. Claudio gave me his phone number. He's a friend; I hang out at his shop sometimes to talk about cars. And I told him, "Hey, man, our singer left, he quit." And he said, "Hey, well, I just talked to Sammy today and he's coming to town." So he gave me Sammy's number and I called him up.

GW: What was Sammy's reaction to the call?

VAN HALEN: He said, "Wow, this could be something!" He wanted to come down to meet us first and see what kind of condition we were in. Because he'd heard some horror stories about my being...way out there, a space case. And he came down and said everything he heard through—well, I won't name any names—but he said, "Man, what's with those people? Why are they talking dirt about ya?"

He came down with Ed Leffler, his manager [*now manager of Van Halen*]. We said, "Hey, we want a band, we don't just want to do a project with you. We want you as a permanent member of the band." First we had a little business meeting, just because he wanted to know what we wanted—to see whether it was like the album he did with Neal Schon, or what. We told him we wanted a permanent member. He came down the next Monday and we jammed, and that was it. The first tune we did was "Summer Nights." And from then on it was just straight up. In 20 minutes we had a complete song.

GW: Was the energy similar to the feeling on *Van Halen*?

VAN HALEN: I can't compare two totally different worlds, totally different atmospheres. Better. In the very beginning, the first album, I was very intimidated by never having been in a studio—it was all new to me. I learned over the years what I want and how to get what I want.

GW: *5150* sounds more crafted than I thought it would be; I expected it to be...

VAN HALEN: Rawer?

GW: But if you examine it, it is the next logical step up from *1984*.

VAN HALEN: I wouldn't say more "crafted"; crafted, to me, sounds like put-together. I'd say it's a little more polished, a little shinier. But not for the purpose of being more mainstream; that just happened to be the music I wrote. And that's the way it transferred to tape. I'm not about to deliberately screw something up to give it an edge. Everything has that garage band energy, but it's polished—we haven't lost that rock and roll soul.

GW: Was it an easy album to make, in terms of putting the songs together and knowing when they were right?

VAN HALEN: A breeze. Beautiful. We never put anything down and then decided to change it. We'd write a tune, put it down, and say, "Yeah, that's it." We might've edited a few spots if a part was too long, but the elements were there.

GW: Some time ago, you said you knew that whatever you did would be judged by what you had done. Did this make you nervous when you were recording *5150*?

VAN HALEN: Oh, sure, it gave us all a little more *ooomph*. Made us try a little harder.

GW: With regard to the session, were the keyboard parts recorded before the guitars?

VAN HALEN: Yes, I did all the keyboards first, alone, and then Al put down drums and Mike overdubbed bass. And then I overdubbed guitar. On "Love Walks In," I played by myself without a beat at all. Seriously. Ask Donn. It was tough for Al but I wasn't that far off. I wanted the chorus part to retard a little bit, and you can't do that with a click track—it would've sounded too robot-like. So Donn and I said, "Forget it, we'll just wing it," and Al managed to play to it. "Dreams" was done with a click track. I used an old 1912 Steinway 7-foot B Grand MIDIed to an Oberheim OB-8.

GW: Is that an acoustic guitar at the beginning of "Dreams"?

VAN HALEN: Yeah. It's a new Kramer Ferrington acoustic guitar with a thin body and an electric guitar neck on it. They sent me the first one. It sounded great, so I had to use it on something.

GW: Did you use the Steinberger guitar on the album?

VAN HALEN: Yeah, with the Trans-Trem. I used that on "Summer Nights" and "Get Up." It's an amazing guitar. You can hit a whole chord with a whammy bar and it will go up or down in tune with itself. So "Get Up" sounds like I'm playing slide, but I'm actually using the wiggle stick.

GW: You were initially wary of the guitar, I understand.

VAN HALEN: Well, that was because I'm used to a piece of wood, and this thing is like plastic. It was kind of alien to me. I had to change a few things to make it sound right. For instance, I had to use my amp differently—I had to use a bassier input. But I talked to Ned [*Steinberger*], and he made some different pickups. They're still EMGs, but they're a little warmer-sounding than the ones he sent to me.

GW: I noticed that the solos on the record sound kind of angry.

VAN HALEN: Angry? Maybe subconsciously, I don't know. But I think they're just sleazy. Kind of slimy-sounding—you never know where they're going to go. They just slip and slide. It's like the old "fall down the stairs and hope you land on your feet" thing. Whatever fits.

GW: Yet the solo on "Love Walks In" is so lyrical.

VAN HALEN: Yeah, I planned that out. I had a melody in my head and it happened to fit. So I said, "What the hell? I might as well use it."

GW: Does Sammy play any guitar on *5150*?

VAN HALEN: No, I played all the guitars. Live, though, he does the solos on the keyboard tunes.

GW: Years ago, didn't Ted Templeman want Sammy Hagar to be Van Halen's singer?

VAN HALEN: I remember hearing something like that. The thing is, Dave has always hated Sammy. I never understood why. We did some shows together—the Oklahoma Jam, and Anaheim Stadium with Black Sabbath and Sammy Hagar—and I always went over and said hi to Sammy because I dug him from his Montrose days. And Dave would always talk shit about him: "Ahhh, that little mother, he ain't got nothin' on me." And I'd wonder, "Where's that even coming from? Why the animosity?" And what Dave says is true— they never even met. Sammy never said a bad word about Dave until Dave started saying shit about him in the English press. I never knew where he was coming from; probably a slight case of jealousy.

GW: I wonder what Van Halen would have been like with Hagar as the original singer?

VAN HALEN: Ummmm, I can't speculate. Maybe Sammy would be doing a movie right now, and Dave would be in the band. [*laughs*] You never know. Seeing how Sammy is blonde, too, we—Alex, Mike and I—figured our purpose was to make lead singers into actors, movie stars. It's just a joke.

GW: *5150* is your first Number One album—how does it feel?

VAN HALEN: It shows me that music overpowers bullshit. Dave and I wrote a lot of good stuff and made a lot of good music together, but I guess the clowning and the show biz part of it only works and helps so much. What's on that tape is what counts. Bottom line. And our going Number One proves that.

GW: Then you think that coming off a huge album like *1984* would not have ensured success had you made a poor album?

VAN HALEN: It would have bombed. But I think we made a good record—a solid record. There's not a song on there I don't like. On previous records there were tunes like "Dancing in the Streets." Come on! That's not me. A funny thing, though: We've played it live—on guitar. Just for fun. We did that in South America when we toured. Maybe if I'd played it on guitar on the record it would have been better. The riff on the record actually was taken from a song of my own, that I was in the midst of writing. Ted heard it and said, "Hey, let's use it for that."

GW: Looking back, what moments stand out for you? Was *1984* one of the high points?

VAN HALEN: It was both a very high and a very low point, emotionally, for me. Since it was recorded at my house, I got a lot of flak from producers and from Dave. In a way, that made me work harder, and in a way, it turned me off to working with those people. So what I did was work at night after everyone split, and then the next day play stuff for them. They're the type of people who, I guess, like to work from noon to 6 p.m., break for dinner, go to sleep at 11, and wake up at noon again. You know what I mean? I'm not that type of person. And they knew that all along. So I guess it scared the crap out of 'em when I built the studio. Because, hey, I'd wake up at five a.m. and want to play. If an idea pops in my head, I want to put it down. You don't put off an idea until tomorrow. I basically wanted to work when I wanted to work, or when I *could* work. I can't just flick a switch on like Dave obviously can. I can't do it that way—at least not creatively.

GW: But after *1984* came out and they saw what you were capable of, wouldn't they allow you more control?

VAN HALEN: I don't know. I think it scared them more. I don't think they were ready to work with me under those conditions again. I think it was that, along with getting rid of our manager, that made Dave just say, "Well, screw you guys, I'm taking off, too." But we didn't do anything wrong. Alex and Mike and I were just sitting there saying, "Whoa! I thought we were doing great. What the hell is going on?" Here was Noel, our manager, suing us. What happened was, he wanted to renegotiate. He sent us a letter saying, "I want more money." We said, "Let's negotiate," but he wouldn't accept our offer. So we didn't fire him, he quit. And since Dave and he were so tight, so to speak, when Noel split he must have really felt he had no more control over me, Alex and Mike. Particularly since Al and I started opening our mouths for a change and were sticking up for what we thought was right. *1984* proved we were right, and so did this new one—not that we were even out to prove anything.

GW: *5150* has more keyboards than any album you've ever done, and it's been the most successful.

VAN HALEN: And what's funny is that Dave was basically against keyboards. Like Billy Gibbons and his, "Hey, you're a guitar hero, nobody wants to see you play keyboards." They had a mental block.

We never even got together long enough to see what he would have come up with for the stuff I was writing. He was too busy doing interviews for his solo career when we had a record to make. He'd call up and say in a gravelly voice, "Ah, I can't make it today, man," and I'd call the office and he'd be doing interviews.

GW: What did you think of *Crazy from the Heat*?

VAN HALEN: I think it was a novelty item. He didn't write any of it—it's full of songs written by other people. In my mind that's an easy way out, because the songs he did have been hits already. Ted has always said, "Hey, when you redo a hit you're halfway there, because the song's been proven." But that's not my way of thinking; I like to do my stuff. That isn't to say I like my own stuff better. But if you have ideas, why be a bar band—why not take a shot at your own stuff? I had enough of playing other people's music in clubs for seven years. Now that I have the chance, I want to do my own.

GW: You made a Number One album with no videos.

VAN HALEN: Yeah, that's true. The reason was that we didn't have time to do even one. And on top of that, my main reason was that since Van Halen used to do such extravagant, loony videos, I didn't want people judging the new face in the band and the new unit by what they saw on some script. I wanted people to see us as we are on stage first. After it was known what we were about, then we could goof off and do whatever we wanted in videos.

Warner Bros. and everyone else wants a video out of us. Our next single is going to be "Dreams." We won't have the time to do a video for that unless we do a live one, so that's probably what we'll have to do. Live is actually the best way to go—it presents us the way we are, not engaged in doing some goofy stuff. The goofy stuff is fun to do, but we didn't want people to get their first impression of us that way.

GW: Do you see yourself doing some outside producing?

VAN HALEN: Sammy asked me to produce his next solo album. And it's going to be fun. I dig working with Sammy, it's great. We come up with stuff so quickly, it's incredible. And he can step out a little and do all kinds of stuff—like writing folk tunes on acoustic guitar. Show a side of himself other than the Red Rocker.

GW: Will the next album show that side?

VAN HALEN: Yeah. One thing Sammy's record won't be is anything like Van Halen. I'm not going to write or play on it; I'll just produce. Because if I write and play, it would sort of sound like Van Halen. And it's not a Van Halen record. I don't want anyone to have the impression that it is—or that he left the band and we're looking for another singer.

GW: Speaking of outside projects, did anything ever come of your desire to work with Pete Townshend?

VAN HALEN: I feel really bad about that. I think Pete Townshend is really pissed off at me. We talked—actually he never called—but he sent telegrams. I tried calling him back, and he telegrammed to say he doesn't like to work in the States, that he wanted to work in England. That kind of threw me a curve, because I was kind of planning to do it in the studio at home. But that wasn't the main reason. He wouldn't have been able to start until November of last year because he was doing his book and his solo album [*White City*]. I was tired of waiting to do something. Also, here are Alex and Mike, who I love, and who are my friends, and who I've been with for years—I couldn't exactly just leave them out. Pete and I never really discussed how to approach the thing, whether it would be Alex and Mike and me or what. I just hope he's not mad at me because I never got hold of him to tell him, "Sorry, I can't do it." I lost his number. I tried to call Phil Chen, who originally got the number for me, and I lost his number, too. You know what a slob I am. I write something down on a matchbook and I light a cigarette and throw the pack away. So Pete, if you read this: I apologize.

GW: Weren't you also trying to work with Patty Smythe?

VAN HALEN: I actually hit her up to possibly join the band and be our lead singer. I just bounced the idea off her. She wasn't sure she could deal with three guys, or something along those lines. And she has a happening solo trip.

Another thing that was bounced around was doing a record with me writing all the music and getting different singers—Joe Cocker, Phil Collins, Mike Rutherford—a different vocalist on each track. But Alex talked me out of it. He said that would be just a one-shot project, and it made me realize, "Yeah, I want a family, I want a solid thing."

The thing is, I never thought Dave would quit—I thought he'd wake up. The things that he said were so weird. He asked how long the album was going to take, his attitude was [*mimics sarcastic tones*], "Hey, man, I've got better things to do, how long is it going to take?" I told him to count on about a year from starting point to album release—writing for a couple of months, recording for three months, and then all the red tape crap of mastering, album covers, T-shirts and all that. And he put it in the press like I just wanted to rot in the studio for a year. We recorded this album in three-and-a-half months—we started in November and by March were on tour for nine months. And he told the press that these so-called "married men" with their Lamborghinis didn't want to tour, but only wanted to do some summer shows. He was the one who suggested not doing a record and just cashing in on the summer circuit. And I said, "What? I don't want to go on tour without any record." He said, "Hey, man, it don't matter." I said we had to do a new record.

The thing is, he's more into money than I am. I'm into making music; I'm a musician. And I love people liking what I'm doing. He's the businessman, not me.

GW: How has Donn responded to the new face?

VAN HALEN: Actually, it was Donn who said, "This is it." Seriously, that one Monday night we jammed, we played for 20 minutes and Donn flicked the talk-back button and said, "I never heard you guys sound that good."

GW: Even Michael and Alex's sound has improved.

VAN HALEN: Oh, yeah, it's a new fire. I'm not saying we couldn't have done a good record with Dave, but I think he started believing the attitude he started copping, the "Hey, I'm God" syndrome. To the point where his hat wouldn't fit his head anymore. I was still willing to put up with it.

GW: I'm curious: How did Valerie respond to all this?

VAN HALEN: She was pissed off, too, because she knew I wanted to quit years ago when we were doing *Fair Warning*. He used to pull shit on her, telling me, "Tell your old lady not to say this and that in the press about you." Bullshit stuff. I said, "Hey, I'm normal, and whatever you are, you are. Don't tell my wife not to say the way I am." I could write a book about the stuff that went down, and none of it had anything to do with music. The guy just did not treat anybody like a human. He was like Idi Amin or Qaddafi.

GUITAR WORLD, JULY 1988

ED, EDDIE, EDWARD

Good buddy, guitar virtuoso, perfectionist: three faces with a single purpose—producing the Van Halen signature sound.

By John Livzey

T HE 5150 COMPLEX lies at the end of a rutted private road, on a wooded hillside rising out of the San Fernando Valley. The hills here are swarming with rock stars, most of whom keep their gates closed. But not this rock star—not now, anyway. There's been a steady stream of traffic in and out of 5150 of late, and the guys in the clubhouse are too busy to be buzzing the gate open every 10 minutes. There are movies to watch on the big-screen TV, pinball games to be played on Captain Fantastic, video battles to be waged on Asteroids, Tempest and Omega Race, hoops to be shot at the NBA-approved basketball goal affixed to the wall of the studio ("Hey, man—keep that ball away from my Lamborghini—please!") and...oh, yeah, there's a Van Halen album to be finished, as soon as Ed, Al, Mike, Sammy, Donn and the guys who work for them get up to cruising speed.

Driving past the gate, you immediately notice that Van Halenland is divided into two distinct parts. On the right side of the driveway is Valerie Villa, with its impeccably maintained estate house, dark-blue-painted swimming pool, well-groomed pets and an air of understated elegance.

On the left side—further on up the road, as it were—is Boys

Town, which houses the recording studio, with its myriad of manly diversions, discarded burrito wrappers and bunches of guys in various stages of busyness. Upstairs is the Edward Van Halen Guitar Showroom (formerly Mrs. Van Halen's exercise room). It's so jam-packed with axes and other weaponry that there just isn't enough room for all of it. Some of Eddie's junk—the guitar synth he never plays, for instance—lies abandoned in a corner. Within the messy confines of his citadel, Van Halen can be himself and do what he does best: write/arrange/produce/play rock and roll music, and be a regular guy—just like all the regular guys he surrounds himself with.

As I pull up to 5150 at high noon, Eddie Van Halen stands by the studio door, grinning that puckish, lopsided, puffy-eyed grin of his. He leads me into the control room, sits in a swivel chair and places an ashtray on the butt-strewn floor between us.

First things first: What does he like to be called?

"Ed, Eddie, Edward—I don't give a damn," he answers, punctuating his words with a snicker. "I used to care—I don't anymore. When I'd introduce myself to people as 'Edward Van Halen,' they'd go, 'Who?' So I'd go, 'Eddie Van Halen.' 'Oh, yeah, sure!' So a lot of times I call myself Eddie now. Al calls me 'Ed'; I call Al 'Al'; my mom calls him 'Alex'...I dunno."

Ed/Eddie/Edward laughs a lot, and his hands are always busy. When he talks about playing the guitar, his fingers move over invisible frets; when he makes a point, he taps you on the knee, good buddy-style. Not only does he play the guitar rhythmically, he moves and speaks according to some internally generated tempo. The guy emits a constant beat.

Van Halen seems entirely too unpretentious to be a mega-celeb—but then you realize that he has carefully arranged his world so that it is possible for him to behave approximately like a normal human being and do his work in surroundings he considers comfortable. Here's a man who can afford the lifestyle of the richest and most famous, and he's chosen the clubby, chummy, sort of cruddy surroundings of his clubhouse. The studio is crammed with the most sophisticated audio gear on the planet, but there's a layer of dust and ashes over everything. Ed wouldn't have it any other way.

"Hey, it's a grungy place and it gets a grungy sound," he says. "That's just the way I like it—down and dirty." Forgetting about the ashtray, I toss a butt on the floor and stamp it out. "Hey, I can do that—you can't!" Ed says in mock-admonition, then laughs uproariously.

"C'mere, you little shit!" commands a familiar female voice, startling Van Halen. It's Valerie Bertinelli, all right, but she's not in the control room—we see and hear her on the surveillance video monitor, as she reprimands one of her cats. Ed looks relieved. A moment later, Mrs. Van Halen pokes her gorgeous head through the door to tell her hubby she's going to run some errands, and he assures her that he's hard at work—first the interview, then the session. She gives him a beatific smile and goes on her way.

According to bassist Mike Anthony, "It's weird, because Valerie comes back here periodically, and it never fails—every time she comes back here, we're in the other room either watchin' TV or playing video games."

What they're supposed to be doing is making a record. Since last October, the members of Van Halen Mach II and longtime engineer/co-producer Donn Landee have been coming up here to record what the principals consider a critical album in the life of this group. Even though 5150—the first effort featuring replacement frontman Sammy Hagar—sold better than any previous VH album, the boys in the band attribute a lot of those sales to mere consumer curiosity. It isn't that they aren't proud of it—they regard the album as a big win by an underdog—but the members of VH II still feel like they've got something to prove. The new release, OU812 (around here, they just call it "the rock and roll album"), is the first one to be undertaken with Hagar as the "throat" as well as Edward's lyricist/collaborator. (Ed, Al and Mike were already working up the material for 5150 when the Roth-to-Hagar transition took place.) It's also the first opportunity for this modified and newly inspired band to show what it can do as a road-tested unit. To hear the players talk, you'd think they were the Oakland Raiders of the Madden era: a bunch of free spirits who broke all the rules and still won the Super Bowl—brash outlaws who regard victory (read: mega-sales) as the ultimate form of vindication (take that, Dave).

And, like the Raiders, they see themselves as macho guys with sensitive sides. On my follow-up visit to 5150, Hagar, a hippie to the core, spends a half-hour waxing poetic about the unfettered joys of Cabo San Lucas, the Baja resort town where he recently bought a condo. Hagar's already fantasizing about sitting au naturel on some secluded, rocky point in Baja, fishing and suckin' down the brewskis. "I'm countin' the days, man," he assures me. "As soon as this is over, I'm outta here." Hagar was inspired to write a song lyric about his love affair with the place, and "Face Down in Cabo (Cabo Wabo)" is being mixed by Landee this very afternoon.

Al, Ed, Mike and several techies and roadies are sitting in the rec room watching *Dragnet: The Movie* on the big screen while they wait for Donn to complete a rough mix in the adjacent control room. After working out on Captain Fantastic, Sammy goes next door to see how "Cabo" is coming along.

The sentimental Anthony pulls me aside to tell me how excited he was after the first-take recording of *5150's* "Summer Nights"— the moment everyone knew without a doubt that Hagar was their boy. "Donn played it back, and we were just all looking at each other—tears practically coming out of everybody's eyes. 'Whoa—this is gonna be something big! This is gonna happen!' It made the fur rise, y'know?" he confides, holding up his forearm for my inspection.

Moments later, Hagar bursts into the room. "You gotta hear this, man—it's awesome!" he says to Eddie, who is seated on a couch. "Look!" the singer demands, holding his arm in front of Eddie's face and pointing at it, exactly as Anthony had done with me. "I showed Donn," Hagar continues, "and he said, 'Me, too!' " Apparently, the success of this album will be measured in terms of sales, airplay and erect body hair.

Suddenly, a monstrous sound erupts from the studio—Landee is playing back a rough mix, and he has cranked it up high enough to knock the squirrels from the trees. I hurry next door to get the full effect. Sitting at the console, the ordinarily pallid Landee has an aerobic flush in his cheeks as the monumental roar of "Cabo Wabo" shakes the building.

Van Halen stands in the doorway, motioning me toward him with a tilt of his head. He has to shout in my ear to make himself heard: "Donn doesn't want anyone else in the room when he's mixing." Oops. Feeling more like an interloper than an interviewer, I hustle out the door. During the track's breathtaking solo section, I watch Edward, his eyes flashing, pace the driveway with the feverish relentlessness of a leopard stalking its next victim. If the music is making his fur rise, he's not acknowledging it. I get the distinct feeling I'm not supposed to be hearing this yet—that Van Halen will serve no vinyl before its time. As the final note decays, he turns on his heels and walks back into the rec room.

During this brief sequence of events, I have a startling revelation: There are three Van Halens. The EVH who's known to the outside world is Eddie the rock star—the grinning dervish you see onstage and in pictures. Then there's Ed the good bud—a snickering, wisecracking everyman who exudes regular-guyness to his pals, who's no more ostentatious than a clump of dirt. But these two are subordinate to Edward the smoldering perfectionist—hermetic, protective, formidable. When push comes to shove in this band, enter Edward, a demanding leader with a killer instinct, accepting no less than optimum effort and absolute loyalty from his subordinates. Eddie mugs for the camera; Ed pokes his buddies in the ribs over dumb jokes in bad movies; Edward is a solipsistic wizard who coaxes supernatural sounds and rhythms from a piece of wood with six strings stretched across it.

Van Halen may come off as happy-go-lucky and just one of the guys, but behind his happy-face mask lie the cognitive/intuitive intricacies of an introspective artist who sets impossible goals for himself and unfailingly achieves them. Clearly, this man still has something to prove—not to the world, but to himself. More than virtuosity, it's his hair-raising ferocity of spirit that separates him from his imitators. The truth is, Edward Van Halen is the king of this

hill—everything else is just jape.
So tell us, Ed—what makes Edward tick?

GUITAR WORLD: I don't intend to dwell on the David Lee Roth issue—that's been done to death.
EDWARD VAN HALEN: Good!
GW: I'm primarily interested in understanding how you make your music. When you play in a trio, like you did for years...
VAN HALEN: Like I'm still doing—a trio with a throat.
GW: When you're playing with just a bass, guitar and drums, every element is crucial, but the guitarist carries most of the load.
VAN HALEN: You gotta fill up the gaps. That's why I always used to use an Echoplex—it made a lot of noise, so it covered up a lot of shit! [*laughs*]
GW: What you do—and what any really good guitarist does in a trio context—is play the spaces as much as the notes. And one of the things that's a hallmark of your style is the clipping of notes, which adds another level of rhythm. Sometimes it sounds fugue-like, almost—like a Bach harpsichord. You started on classical music, didn't you?
VAN HALEN: Oh yeah, I was classically trained on piano up until I was 12.
GW: But the first guitar you played was a flamenco guitar, right?
VAN HALEN: Yeah, a nylon-string job.
GW: There are a couple of things on your albums that demonstrate quite a bit of dexterity on the nylon-string; "Spanish Fly" is one of them. It's neat to hear that kind of attack on such a delicate-sounding instrument.
VAN HALEN: It's sort of a funny thing how that happened. I think it was New Year's Eve back in '78 or '79. Alex and I were over at [*producer*] Ted Templeman's house, and there was this acoustic guitar sittin' in the corner. I started fooling around on it, y'know—I had half a beat going, and I said, "Mmmm, I feel like jamming a little bit." Ted walks in and he said, "Wow, you can play acoustic guitar?" I looked at him like, "What's the difference? It's got six strings—it's a

guitar!" So I ended up coming up with "Spanish Fly."

GW: Did you play a lot of acoustic guitar around the house?

VAN HALEN: In the very, very beginning I did, because I couldn't afford an electric one.

GW: Did you usually have an acoustic around, or did you just sort of go and become a lap player? You know what I mean by that?

VAN HALEN: A lap player?

GW: Yeah, you sit on your bed, you put the guitar on your lap and you play.

VAN HALEN: Oh yeah! On the bed.

GW: On the bed, in the motel room.

VAN HALEN: Yeah, I did that for years, man.

GW: So what was your first electric guitar?

VAN HALEN: It was a Teisco Del Rey. Actually, I have a similar one upstairs.

GW: Three pickups?

VAN HALEN: Four pickups. It's funny, because now I use one.

GW: You've been quoted as saying that you got your initial licks from Clapton, off the first Bluesbreakers album. Was that the case?

VAN HALEN: Actually, I was totally into Cream, and then I started digging back and buying all the John Mayall stuff.

GW: Your solo tone has always been really reminiscent of Clapton's— the tone he got by playing with his pick and then hitting the string with the top of his nail: doubling. I can see where the hammer-ons and all that evolved from that technique.

VAN HALEN: I use my thumb and my middle finger when I pick. Actually, it depends. Normally, I pick like that, but when I do the hammer-on stuff I hold it this way [*wedges the pick between the first and second joints of his middle finger*]. A lot of people say, "Hey whaddaya do with your pick?"—because they don't see it. It's just right there. You see a lot of people stick the pick between their teeth, and I just had to figure out something else. And sometimes, when I use the wiggle stick, I hold it with my pinky and pick like that [*holds the pick between his thumb and index finger, with the last three fingers slightly curled to form a fulcrum for the bar*], and pick the Mel Bay style—

the way you're supposed to, up and down, up and down. See, my bar is so loose that I don't have to keep these fingers straight.

As far as the hammer-on thing is concerned—I never really saw anybody do it, okay? I'm not saying, "Hey, I'm bitchin', I came up with it," but I never really saw anybody do it. But I got the idea a long time ago when I saw Led Zeppelin, back in '71 or something like that. Page was doing his guitar solo before "Heartbreaker," or in the middle of it [*hums guitar riff*]. He stood there playing [*hums some more*], and I think, "Wait a minute, open string, pull off. I can do that. Use that finger up here, and use this as the nut, and move it around." That's how I first thought of it, and I don't know if anyone else did it. I just kind of took it and ran with it. People say, "Holy shit, man, you do it all over the place now, instead of just using open strings."

GW: When did you integrate the technique into your style?

VAN HALEN: Put it this way: since even before we started doing original tunes. I think I was actually doing that before I ever wrote a tune. I remember when we first started playing original sets, at the Whisky or Starwood, I'd turn around when I did it, because Al said, "Hey guys, be cool. Don't let those mothers rip you off!"

GW: To return to playing in a three-piece context: Even when not playing strict rhythm—as you rarely do—good guitarists make the rhythmic stuff happen.

VAN HALEN: I always felt that I was a rhythmic kind of player—I mean, in my leads. I have a weird sense of time. A lot of times I'll count something off, or I'll just start playing something, and Al will come in completely backwards from the normal beat. It's almost a running joke in the band. I don't do it on purpose; I just kind of never come in on the "one."

GW: Your playing, on record, has an extreme blockbuster intensity that I suppose has to do, to a certain extent, with Donn Landee and his engineering. But how do you make it sound so "atomic bomb"?

VAN HALEN: That's Donn, man, I don't know.

GW: When you're working, you do a lot of first—and second—take solos.

VAN HALEN: Oh, definitely. Nothing is really planned out. I don't know how to explain it, but when Donn gets here, talk to him for a minute. If you ask him, "How do you do what you do?" he'll say, "I don't know." I swear to God. Sometimes when Donn tries to think something out, it doesn't work. He'll just throw a couple of mics out there and get a unique kind of thing happening. You can't learn it at Columbia School of Broadcasting—you know what I mean?

GW: Is it that anything could work in a given situation—he has an idea, and you have an idea, they just come together and it works?

VAN HALEN: It's kind of a magic that happens; nothing is really calculated.

GW: That's one problem with trying to explain artistry: Artists are the last ones who can explain it.

VAN HALEN: Take my guitar sound—I don't think we've changed the way we mike. I've got a Shure 57 or 58 right up on the speaker; it's the only way I've ever miked my amp! We never try in a big room, a little room or far-miking or anything—just a mic right up.

GW: I read recently about your Bradshaw rack, and thought, "Where does he use it? Where is it?"

VAN HALEN: I really don't use it.

GW: You got it because you can have one, but you don't use it. I hear DDL, a little phase, chorus, flanging—but it still sounds to me like a DiMarzio pickup or whatever it is pushing the Marshall amplifier. You get a lot of air.

VAN HALEN: I go straight into my amp. When we're done here I'll show you what I use.

GW: Have you recorded anything that mainly depended on an effect?

VAN HALEN: Two things: MiniMoog on "Dancing in the Streets," because I didn't know what sequencers were or anything like that, so I just played the riff and added an echo; and "Cathedral," same thing—same record, as a matter of fact. I was in that echo mode. Those two things I couldn't do without the echo.

GW: Would you say "Eruption" represents the crystallization of your approach to playing guitar? It's almost like a textbook study of your technique, and it's the number that led a million guitarists to think,

"Wow, I gotta figure out how he did that." And they still want to know. But maybe there isn't any secret to it.

VAN HALEN: There ain't—not that I know of. What do you mean? What kind of secrets?

GW: What do you think of Stanley Jordan?

VAN HALEN: I respect him—I've seen him on the Johnny Carson show, seen him do his thing—but to me, what he's doing is eliminating other band members. He's taking tapping to the point where it's like more than one person playing; whereas I don't care to get into it that far. To me, it's just an extension of the way I play guitar—not, "Well, I want to play the bass, too." To me, that's so out there that it's like computerized shit, almost. Someone will hear it and go, "Wow, it sounds great," but it is so beyond that it's almost not special—I don't know how to explain it.

GW: Does it have to do with the idea that when you play with a band—a drummer and a bass player—you're working off the energy of the other guys as well as your own?

VAN HALEN: Oh yeah. There's a guessing game going on all the time, and there's the friction, a feeling of being on the edge of your seat—who's going to fall, who's gonna lose it first? It creates excitement. Whereas if you're doing it all yourself, it sounds like a guy with a drum machine and a sequencer, blowing a sax to it or something.

GW: In a way, the rock band is like an endangered species now because of that technology. Kids who are learning how to play now have the sequencers and the computers and stuff, but they lack the interaction.

VAN HALEN: That reckless abandon of falling down the stairs and hoping to land on your feet.

GW: So you are doing God's work here, in a way, by inspiring people to fall down those stairs. To a certain extent, *5150* breaks with the pattern of your first six albums in the sense that, as you described in an earlier interview, you started tracks with keyboards, and also in that you take a more constructed approach.

VAN HALEN: The reason being that that room isn't big enough for us to play drums and piano and mike 'em both at the same time! It wasn't on purpose. As soon as we're done with this record, I'm going to knock that back wall out and build another room to put the piano in. I was going crazy, telling Al, "Damn, I wish I could play at the same time with you," but I couldn't, because miking the piano and miking the drums didn't work in the same room.

GW: But why not overdub the keyboards?

VAN HALEN: What's Al going to play to? The piano is the melody.

GW: So what do you do, put a click down?

VAN HALEN: No, uh-uh. No click, I just played the piano, MIDIed to my OB-8.

GW: So you dictate the time with your innate sense of rhythm—and nothing else. Did you ever check it metronomically against real time?

VAN HALEN: No, I just go by what feels right.

GW: Is that the way you're working on this album as well?

VAN HALEN: Yeah. This time around, there hasn't been a song yet where I play first and Al overdubs.

GW: How's it working this time?

VAN HALEN: Well, I haven't used the piano yet. I'm using synthesizers, but they're direct so there's no problem with bleed. There's one song where I overdubbed the piano. It's a pretty rocking album— there's no wimpy shit here. It's not necessarily back to basics, but it's rawer. We're actually out there playing live again. It's more a loose kind of trip. I remember that after we did *5150*, we said to each other, "Next record we're really going to put it together right." Instead it's the other way around!

GW: Wasn't *5150* put together with less abandon?

VAN HALEN: Only "Love Walks In" and "Dreams," because those were the piano tunes. They had to be thought out.

GW: In terms of overall ambiance, "Why Can't This Be Love?" sounds like the most elaborate Van Halen song ever.

VAN HALEN: It's because of the instrumentation. I used the arpeggiator in the OB-8, so everyone had to play to that. That's why it has kind of a uniform effect.

GW: It sounds much more polished.

VAN HALEN: It's more pop-popular, right? If more people like it, it's pop, right? What's wrong with that? I would love to have written a Christmas carol. What's wrong with that?

GW: Do you ever feel limited by the specific demands of your audience? As in, "Maybe my public won't like it if there aren't at least three hammer-on solos."

VAN HALEN: I don't think so. I'll do anything that I feel like doing. I have to like it. And if I like it, that's all that matters. I mean, it's kind of a stuck-up attitude maybe, but I really believe that I have to like it before I can even attempt to have anyone else like it.

GW: What was your first serious guitar?

VAN HALEN: I had a gold-top Les Paul with soap-bar pickups.

GW: The thing about a Les Paul is, it always sounds like a Les Paul. No matter how much you try, you can't get it to sound like anything else. But when you play a Stratocaster-style guitar, you have to work at it harder.

VAN HALEN: I never understood the difference—I can't tell. As a matter of fact, when I pick up a Paul now it's probably harder for me.

GW: The Les Paul neck, to me, feels more like an acoustic guitar, whereas a Stratocaster...

VAN HALEN: It was never this hand [*holds up his left hand*] that bothered me on any guitar; it was the other side, because the bridge on the Les Paul is higher, and I always rest the palm of my hand on the bridge—when I play a muffle, for example.

GW: What about the gauge of the strings?

VAN HALEN: I went through all kinds of phases. Just like with picks— I still don't know what I like. Sometimes I use fat ones, sometimes thin ones. String-wise, for a long time I used real heavy ones because I tuned way down to like D-flat, C-sharp.

GW: You've even used a bass string.

VAN HALEN: Oh yeah. That's kind of cool—an A and an A bass string.

GW: And then that gets you into different tunings, too, I guess. So how do you figure that stuff out?

VAN HALEN: I think the only tune I've ever really used a strange tuning on was "Top Jimmy" on *1984*. I had this melody in my head and figured I'd just tune to the melody.

GW: In that case, the melody just came into your head. Does it usually come to you that effortlessly?

VAN HALEN: It takes me forever to write. I have to like something—I hate just puking something out. I could probably write you five tunes in the time we're here, but they'd be bullshit to me. You might like 'em, I don't know, but I have to like something. I don't please myself very easily, I guess. And it's not like a perfectionist kind of thing.

GW: Do you know where they come from, the ideas? Do they just kind of pop into your head? Or do they pop into your fingers first?

VAN HALEN: A lot of times, yeah. Sammy has this theory—his three-lock-box theory—where spiritually, mentally and physically, you gotta be together in order for anything creative to really happen. He had a song called "Three Lock Box," which a lot of people thought was about…[*runs his right index finger in and out of his left fist*] you know? It ain't—it's a pretty heavy thing. Actually, I agree with it. You can have an idea in your head, but if you can't execute it, what's the use? You got to have the technical shit down. That's what I mean when I say that it comes from your fingers sometimes. You'll be playing and, all of a sudden, you'll have an idea in your head and your fingers will just go with it. And the more you do that, and the more you listen to other things, something's bound to filter through and come out.

GW: Do you practice a lot?

VAN HALEN: It depends on what you call practicing. I never sat down and learned scales, or said, "Oh wow, now I'm going to play a minor scale." What I do is, I just noodle; that's all I do—noodle.

GW: You mean you just sit all the time with a guitar in your hands?

VAN HALEN: Exactly. I just noodle.

GW: So your attitude about what you really do, which is play the guitar—that's what you really do fundamentally, because everything else springs from that—hasn't really changed over the years.

VAN HALEN: I guess. You can answer that better than me!

GW: To many people, you're on that Hendrix level—you know, that ultimate rock guy level—and yet you're just the same regular guy you were all along. But there's so much stuff surrounding you—I'm sure many people want a piece of you. How do you deal with that? Have you found a way to insulate yourself from all that attention and ado-ration?

VAN HALEN: Maybe I don't deal with it, that's why I...

GW: But you've managed to not be changed by it, which is the key.

VAN HALEN: Well, I don't see how it can change someone, I really don't.

GW: But you see where it does change people, though.

VAN HALEN: Oh, I've seen people close to me change, you know? But I don't understand why. A lot of people, all they want is the fame. I'll take the fortune, you can have the fame. [*laughs*]

GW: A fortune only allows you the freedom to do what you wanted to do in the first place. But if you become famous, you lose the free-dom to do what you wanted to do.

VAN HALEN: Exactly, it's Catch-22, man—you're screwed no matter what you do. The one thing that keeps me kinda sane, though, is that I don't really know how to be pretentious.

GW: Yeah, I can see that. Do you feel pressure from any particular sector at this point in your life? I'm sure Warner Bros. would like to have a record.

VAN HALEN: There's no pressure, though I guess they do—I don't real-ly think about it. I create my own pressure, though. I'm working on a tune right now, and I'm frustrated to death because I'm stuck. Everyone else says, "It sounds great—what are you worried about?" But something ain't jiving within my head, and I'm frustrated—it pisses me off.

GW: What do you do when you get into a situation like that?

VAN HALEN: I drink a couple of beers, smoke a couple of packs of cigarettes and try and walk away from it for a bit. Then I come back. I'm actually the type of person, though, who doesn't like to stay away. A lot of people think that if you're burnt on something, you should go on to something else and come back to it later. I can't do that. I believe that if you work through it, if you scale that wall, it'll be better than if you come back to it fresh and don't have the same frustrated attitude towards it. Because, when you come back, your attitude toward the song will be different—you're not fighting anymore.

GW: So you use the frustration.

VAN HALEN: In a funny way, I do. But I don't wish it upon anyone, because I don't like it.

GW: But that's part of being an artist.

VAN HALEN: Usually, when the frustration hits and I come through it, I have a better tune than something that came easy.

GW: People have a tendency to rely too much on inspiration as opposed to getting down to it.

VAN HALEN: I think the most frustrated I've probably ever been was with the intro to "Little Guitars," the little flamenco-like thing. This is a prime example of me overcoming this wall. I had this thing in my head, but had trouble with it because I can't fingerpick like that. I wanted to do [*sings guitar riff*].

GW: That's called frailing.

VAN HALEN: Yeah, well whatever, I can't do that. I said, "I gotta put this on a record, because I've got this melody and I wanna do it." So I just took an open E, fanned the thing and did the pull-offs on the low E. Let me show you. [*continues talking while strapping on his 5150 guitar.*] Where there's a will, there's a way, whether you call it cheating or not. The end result is how it sounds, right? [*starts flamenco noodling on guitar.*] I forget exactly how it went. But I remember when we were mastering the record over at Amigo, Warner Bros. Studios, Steve Lukather and the guys were there, listening, and they said, "Wow, I didn't know you could play like that." I said, "I don't." [*laughs*]

GW: I notice that you have the action on this a little higher than on your other guitars, and the strings are a lighter gauge.

VAN HALEN: That's not on purpose—it's mostly because I didn't put it together right. I use .009, .011, .016, whatever—regular slinkies. I'm not real good at setting up guitars.

GW: Look, it's got cigarette burns on it. This is a rock guitar, man.

Frank White

VAN HALEN: [*snickering*] The backside's real nice, too.

GW: You've finally got everything the way you want—you've pretty much solved all the problems you had in the past.

VAN HALEN: Don't get me wrong—I don't think our first six albums were bad or anything. I think we did some good stuff. It's just different now, different chemistry happening—a different quarterback, so to speak, or we're running different plays. We won the Super Bowl last year. And we're gonna be the first ones to do it twice in a row. In my mind, I go by how I feel about what we do, whether we even release it or not. I dig what we're doing, the new stuff...it's inspiring to me. If I write something and when I play it back, my fur rises, that's like, "Whoa, where did that come from?" It's spooky. When I hear something that I did, and I'm not really conscious of the fact that that's me, that blows me away, always. I love that! There are a lot of moments like that on this record.

GW: Can you cite specific moments on past records where you had that feeling?

VAN HALEN: Not right off the bat. There were some solos I did on *Fair Warning* that kind of gave me the chills. That was our worst-selling album to date, the fourth one. It was kind of a dark album—it was a bad time in my life. There's a lot of interesting guitar on it, though.

GW: So you were pulling on the downside of your emotions.

VAN HALEN: You know, you go with what you've got. I wasn't consciously trying to be down. [*laughs*]

GW: The solos are great on that record.

VAN HALEN: It's weird stuff.

GW: Earlier you referred to a problem you've been having with one song.

VAN HALEN: Well, it's only been a problem since yesterday—I just came up with it yesterday, and I'm stuck.

GW: Is that just a song, or is it something that's going to be on this album?

VAN HALEN: I'd like it to be on the record.

GW: So this album isn't completely nailed down yet.

VAN HALEN: Yeah, I'd say we're about two thirds of the way into it. We've got nine tracks, and I always like to have a couple extra. I like to drop the needle at the beginning and listen all the way through, and if something isn't right, I like to be able to say, "Well, maybe this song would make it flow well."

GW: Do you ever say to yourself: "Well, we could use another one of these kind of songs?"

VAN HALEN: No-no-no, I can't do that, because I can't write on demand. I guess some people can. They say, "We need a song like this," and they'll contrive a tune similar to what they think they need. But I can't do that. I don't know how other people write, or where their inspiration or ideas come from. But me, I just have to go with what comes out, which makes it tough sometimes. Sometimes nothing comes out; other times what does come out comes in little spurts, and if I don't go with it right then... Sometimes I'll think, "Aaaah, I'll work on it some more tomorrow," and I'll totally forget what track I was on.

GW: When you first come up with an idea, do you just put it on cassette?

VAN HALEN: Sometimes I'll hum it into a little microcassette. I remember once a few years ago, when we toured down in South America, Valerie was sleeping and I didn't want to wake her up, so I went in the closet. [*laughs*] What it ended up being was "Girl Gone Bad" on *1984*. Oh man, it'd be funny if I could play you the tape, but I don't know where it is.

GW: There must be a certain point where you say, "Okay, I can anticipate the recording of another album, so I've got to get some songs together." Do you try to sort of schedule a time where you write the bulk of the songs, and then...

VAN HALEN: No. See, for one, I don't consider this my career—it's my life. It's not like I go to work, and now I'm going to map out when I'm going to work and stop working. It's just kind of a continuous, round-the-clock thing—whenever it hits, I do it. It's been almost two years since the last record, partly because I just wanted to spend time with the family. Also, I did Sammy's record, and we definitely didn't want a Van Halen record out there at the same time as his. People were saying, "Huh? Is he in Van Halen or what? Who's gonna be the next singer?" No, it's just kind of an ongoing thing. I don't say, "Okay, now I'm gonna write, and stockpile some tunes, so when we record I'll be ready." Actually, I walked in pretty cold this time. I said, "Well, do you want to start?" "Okay, whaddaya got?" "Call me tomorrow!"

GW: But you did get to a point where the ideas were popping out, because you were psyched up.

VAN HALEN: Oh, yeah. I guess when I put my mind in that mode, when the electricity starts happening, it just kind of happens.

GW: Was there a particular song idea that generated a lot of your momentum? The first one that really made sense to you?

VAN HALEN: Yeah, the one I was just starting to play.

GW: The one that started with the keyboard?

VAN HALEN: It's kind of an inspired tune, and it really started the ball rolling.

GW: What's that going to be called?

VAN HALEN: "When It's Love," or "How Do You Know When It's Love?"

GW: There seems to be an element of consistency in the way you approach things. Do you feel like you're a better musician now than you were eight or nine years ago?

VAN HALEN: I don't know. Sometimes I hear an old tune on the radio, and I think, "How did I do that?" Whereas, if it was back then and I were to hear what I'm doing now, I'd probably say the same thing. So I don't know. I think I'm better at executing my ideas.

GW: Do you feel you've reached a certain plateau?

VAN HALEN: Yeah, in a funny way. I used to hit plateaus all the time when it came to riffs, soloing, because I got sick of hanging in the same area with the guitar, trying to squeeze the most out of those same notes. I guess playing keyboards has helped a lot, because now I have another instrument to bozo out on.

GW: So that'll keep you from ultimately getting burned out on the guitar, since you can always go to another instrument. But you're still in the same mindset.

VAN HALEN: Right. I want to learn how to play sax, too. Oh, I love sax. Guitar is actually kind of like sax—like some of the old Cream guitar tones. Allan Holdsworth, he sounds like he's blowin'!

GW: Have you tried a guitar synthesizer?

VAN HALEN: Everyone asks me that. No! I tried one years ago, and it didn't track for shit. And to me, it's like you have to alter your playing for this sound. At least that's what I remember. This was, like, five years ago, when Roland developed them. You can't just plug into it. For one thing, you've gotta play their guitar, you know—I think there's one company that had the thing that slides underneath your pickup—but you can't just play normal guitar and then layer that on top of it. You have to adapt to it, and I don't like that. And besides, I play keyboards; so if I want any kind of fancy shit, I'll just do it with ten fingers. I don't think the guitar synthesizers have really found a spot on this planet.

GW: You don't need it, basically.

VAN HALEN: No, I don't. That's the bottom-line reason I'm not interested. If I want electronic stuff I'll play it on keyboards. Why bastardize the guitar?

GW: How do you know when an idea's gonna relate more to keyboards than to the guitar, and vice versa?

VAN HALEN: When I get an idea in my head, it's either on keyboard or guitar. I guess I come up with different stuff on guitar than on keyboard. But then in the old days I'd come up with riffs, like on "And the Cradle Will Rock," that I played on a Wurlitzer electric piano through my Marshalls, and that was kind of like a guitar riff that I put to keyboard. "Hear About It Later" from *Fair Warning* was actually a piano riff that I put to guitar. I don't know if I'm answering your question, but...

GW: It's just whatever's closer at hand?

VAN HALEN: I have no set approach, because often I'll be sitting around humming a riff and envisioning that on the piano, and other times I'll be humming and I'll be thinking guitar.

GW: It does sound like you're getting a little more systematic about how you approach things.

VAN HALEN: Obviously, once we start a record, there's a schedule. And sometimes we don't meet schedules! [*laughs*] It's like right now, our manager's asking, "When's it gonna be done?" I say, "Damned if I know! When it's done, I'll let you know." I can't do it like that, otherwise I'll puke it out. But then again, I'm not the type of person who really likes to sit there and brew on the stuff for too long either. If I lose interest, forget it.

GW: A song is a series of guitar licks as much as it is verses, choruses and a bridge, right? It all just kind of comes out in this one block of...

VAN HALEN: Well, sometimes it doesn't. Sometimes I'll have just one riff, and then I'll say, "Where do I go from here?"

GW: Now that you've got things set up pretty much the way you want, do you ever think about doing an instrumental album? Or are you getting all the creative satisfaction you need?

VAN HALEN: I think I get my rocks off pretty well. I don't have any deep, hidden things that I want to get out. I do what I do, and everything seems to fit. If I wanna do a long solo, I'll do a long solo—no one's telling me I can't. A lot of the tunes on this record are long, too—so far there's no song under five-and-a-half minutes—and three or four of them are over seven minutes. We'll have to cut them down a little bit. I don't know how we're gonna do that, either.

GW: You guys are usually pretty concise. Even those little intros, and the little connectors between cuts, are like complete ideas in themselves. Do you have anything like that happening on this album?

VAN HALEN: Yeah, there are a couple of little things like that on this one. I don't know, I always like to kinda have something to start off a tune, to set the mood for it.

GW: It can be the intro to the song.

VAN HALEN: They're sort of like little commercials between songs, know what I mean? Like, "Hey, buy Tide, Super-Improved Tide," and then the next song starts. Now that I think about it, the intros that I've done—guitar things like "Cathedral" or "Little Guitars"—really have nothing to do with the song before or after.

GW: How do you warm up?

VAN HALEN: I just pick up the guitar and noodle. Most of the time, what I'm trying to do is write a new tune. I think more in terms of songs than I do riffs. Just doing licks. In the old days, when I first started learning how to play lead, all I'd do is try and figure out little leads. Once you get to the point where you can pretty much execute anything that pops into your head, you start thinking more song, I guess. At least I do. So when I warm up, I just kind of noodle and hum shit in my head. I write probably 90 percent of my tunes on tour—either during soundcheck or warming up for the gig.

GW: That's interesting. I recently spoke with the guys in Squeeze, who told me that in order to write, they had to be at home where they follow a self-imposed regimen.

VAN HALEN: Well, to actually put things down on tape, yeah. But on tour, I'll have the seeds of a hundred songs, and come home and listen to little bitty ideas of things.

GW: On a microcassette?

VAN HALEN: Actually, I've only used the microcassette machine a few times. Usually I remember the idea. But at the same time, out at the beach I got a piano, and a couple of guitars, and if something pops in my head I'll just pick up the guitar and jam, or play piano.

GW: You think pretty much in the standard mode of music, right? You don't deal with weird modalities or...

VAN HALEN: I don't think in terms of scales at all. I just think whatever pops into my head. Like sometimes I do some weird intervals or chord changes, and I hate it when people say "Hey, he just went from a this to a that." So fuckin' what?

GW: I've heard lead guitar described as pattern playing and scale playing.

VAN HALEN: That sounds the same to me. I'm just kind of a "wing it" player.

GW: You're working on a record, and that presupposes dealing with deadline pressure—no matter where you record. But you have your own studio—you can set up a casual schedule, if you want. Do you have to discipline yourself to avoid being overly casual?

VAN HALEN: Here's the thing: Every day we say, "Okay, we'll start at

2:00 tomorrow." And then I'll stay overnight here, or be here by noon, messing around. Sammy shows up at 2:30, Donn gets here at maybe 1:30. Then Mike will get here at 3:00 and go in there and play pinball or goof off until about 4:00. And then we'll leave at 5:30. The next day, Mike'll say, "My car broke down—I gotta take it to the shop. I'll be a little late." And we'll say, "Why don't we just blow it off today?" We actually started recording, I think, in October, one day a month. [*laughs*] Nahh, that's an exaggeration—it was maybe two days a week for a couple hours. One good thing about having Ted around—he really cracked the whip.

GW: But when you get down to it, you must get a lot accomplished if you're able to be that casual about it, yet still wind up with the record you want.

VAN HALEN: Chris [*Pollan*], our tour manager, always says, "You guys, man, you watch television, play a song once, come back, watch television for another hour, play a song once, man...what kinda life is this?" [*laughs*] Because really, in a day, we probably get maybe 45 minutes of work out, and we're here maybe from 2 p.m. to 7 p.m.

GW: So they're not marathon sessions at all. You never do a real long one?

VAN HALEN: Well, it varies. If we're onto something, we'll take it until we're down.

GW: Earlier, you said that you've come to think more in terms of writing rather than playing. When an idea for a song strikes you, what comes first, the melody or the changes? Or does that vary?

VAN HALEN: Usually the melody. Most of the riffs that I come up with, or pieces of music, are melodic little ditties. They're things that I hum in my head and play.

GW: At what stage of development does a musical idea have to be in before you show it to Sammy?

VAN HALEN: I'll have an intro, a verse, a B-section, a chorus and a solo section. I'll pretty much have the parts for a completed song.

GW: Do you put it on tape for him? Do you get it to the stage where you say, "Okay, now it's ready?"

VAN HALEN: No. We cut the tracks when we're all here.

GW: What I mean is, do you put the guitar parts on a cassette?

VAN HALEN: Yeah, I'll either do that or play it for him live. Al and I will play it, with the beat, and then Sammy'll say, "Go here from that point, instead of where you went." I'll try it, and if it works we'll do it. If not...You know, it's a band thing. Whenever you've got four people together, one's bound to not like everything you do. I come up with the parts, though, and we'll either all piece it together or I'll do it myself. It's not really set which way.

GW: Does Sammy ever come in with a lyric and turn the tables?

VAN HALEN: You mean inspire me to write music to the lyric? Not yet.

GW: So far, you've cut eight tracks for the record. Will there be any more?

VAN HALEN: A couple more, yeah. This one today, I hope.

GW: You mean, you just had this idea on Thursday, and on Monday it's going to be recorded?

VAN HALEN: Yeah. Why wait? When things happen, they happen fast. Sammy's got a place down in Cabo, Mexico. He wrote a song called "Cabo Wabo," about being smashed, you know. Anyway, that was done, like, in two days. I came up with it one day; next day we cut it. It came together real quick. Actually, though, I don't really write here. I don't write in the studio. I'll get the ideas either in the house, or at the beach, or wherever I am. Here is where I put it together. I never really come up with the seeds of songs here.

GW: You've got all these electronic distractions here. I guess just being with your guitar and being...

VAN HALEN: That's not necessarily it. I just look at the studio as a place where you put it all together, where you make it a real thing.

GW: Is there a particular place where ideas have often come to you over the years?

VAN HALEN: In bed, right before I fall asleep, I come up with all kinds of shit. Right as I start to drift off.

GW: When you wake up it's still there?

VAN HALEN: Well, not always.

GW: Have you cut any of the solos to the new record yet, or are you waiting?

VAN HALEN: I've done a few, yeah. A lot of 'em are live.

GW: So you're following your usual procedure.

VAN HALEN: Right. Usually, if it's an uptempo kind of rocker, I just blaze through it; whereas if it's a real melodic kind of tune, I like to think out a melodic solo. I'll play a rhythm track and then overdub the solo.

GW: Do you ever splice your solos together?

VAN HALEN: Oh, we've done compilations, sure. Sometimes I'll do three solos, and I'll say, "I like the beginning of that one, I like the end of that one, and I like the middle of that one." Whatever sounds good—there are no rules. And I ain't proud; I don't give a damn if I get it in one take or not! If it gets me off, it's fine.

GW: Whenever I've seen pictures of you playing, in videos or whatever, you always have a big smile on your face. Is that for the camera, or...?

VAN HALEN: No, I'm just having a good time! I'm just a happy guy, I guess. It's funny, because usually, whenever there's a camera in front of my face, I shy away from it. I'm not that kind of guy, you know? I'm not a camera flirt. I'm just kinda grooving, having fun, you know? I'm laughing at something or somebody, or something I did that I got away with. My attitude's always been, "If you can't get out there in your boxer shorts and your axe, you're screwed!"

I arrive at the studio at the agreed-upon time, and Van Halen strides up to my car, probably wondering what I'm doing there. When I explain that Landee has offered me a chance to discuss the completed album, he tells me that only seven of the 10 cuts have been mixed, and that Landee hasn't arrived yet. While I content myself with shooting baskets, the master of the estate ambles back and forth between the clubhouse and Valerie Villa. Ed must be getting in shape for the Monsters of Rock tour—he's now drinking Koala coolers instead of Heineken, and he's smoking Merit Ultra Lights instead of Marlboros (although there are boxes of the latter sitting on various surfaces in the rec room).

When Landee still hasn't arrived by 1 p.m., I start to banter with Ed, hoping to steer the conversation around to the new album. But that isn't necessary—he brings up the subject himself, ebulliently explaining that this is the first album he's made that he can't stop listening to. "It still makes my fur rise," he tells me.

We head into the control room and take a look at the song list, which Landee has written out on a sheet of legal pad. There's a big surprise at the bottom of the page: Van Halen has covered Little Feat's "Apolitical Blues," the original version of which Landee recorded 16 years earlier with Ted Templeman. The tune is slated for the CD and cassette versions of *OU812*, as well as for the B-side of the first single, fronted by "Black & Blue," a heavy, mid-tempo rocker that Ed considers to be the most characteristically Van Halen track on the album.

The album is scheduled to be mastered this Friday, and Ed and Valerie are embarking on their seventh-anniversary vacation on the following Tuesday. Nevertheless, Van Halen is still hedging on the album title. "I just wanna call it *Rock and Roll*," he says, "because that's what it is. It ain't heavy metal, it's not hard rock—it's rock and roll."

So what about the tunes, Ed?

"Now wait a minute," he cautions me, as I began jotting down the song titles on the list. "I wouldn't write the titles down yet. This first one, 'Naturally Wired,' we might call that 'AFU,' because the chorus is 'I'm all fired up.' Then again, the rideout is 'I'm naturally wired.' So it's either 'Naturally Wired,' 'All Fired Up' or 'AFU.' 'Finish What You Started' could be 'Baby Come On,' or 'Come on Baby.' And 'Source' or 'Source of Infection'…"

Is that an AIDS song?

"No-no-no. I first wanted to call the album that. Y'know, Van Halen: *Source of Infection*—'music that's infectious.' Actually, Sammy came up with it, and I saw it that way. Al grossed out. He said, 'Sounds like a sore or somethin'.' I went, 'Okay, screw it.' I mean, we got a list like that of album titles. I don't know why they put *OU812* in that press release. Probably [*VH manager*] Ed Leffler just thought, since that was the latest one we bounced off of him, that's the one we decided on. *Rock and Roll*—I think that's classic. To me, though, an album title or a song title does not sell anything. It's just to let people know you got a new one out. Like Chicago—1-2-3-4-13-15-18… 'Hey—we got a new one.' Who gives a damn what it's called? Call it *Mustard on Your Leg* or something—here's the new one. Call it *Yogurt!*"

I learn that the tune that gave Van Halen difficulties during my first visit to 5150 has become "Feel So Good," which Ed describes as a keyboard-powered pop song. (As I later discover, it's one of this album's most delightful surprises.)

"Yeah, I was kinda stumped on it, but I got past the hump. That one and 'When It's Love' are the most overdubbed songs. 'Apolitical Blues' is totally live except for the piano overdub that I did. It's just a sloppy blues. I tried to play it like [*Little Feat pianist*] Billy Payne. I'm not really that kind of player, but it was tripped-out, man, trying to do these slippery blues licks on piano and land on your feet. We spent like half an hour on it; Donn just hung two overhead mics and that was it. It's so gross-sounding. I played slide on that black Airline guitar, through a little Music Man amp, and got a sound that's almost identical to the one Lowell [*George*] got. It's naaasty."

Ed runs down the song list with his blue Fender medium guitar pick. "I laid direct on 'Baby Come On,' 'Finish What You Started' or 'Come on Baby,'" he says with a snicker. "Al was alone in there," he adds, pointing to the room on the other side of the glass, "so the drums sound real cool. Sammy and I were in here direct [with Hagar strumming an acoustic], and Mike was in here, too, playing. So the three of us are standing here waving, saying, 'Hey Al, having fun out there?'

"Then there's 'Cabo'—that's either 'Face Down in Cabo,' or 'Cabo Wabo.' That one we recorded in a real weird way—the room just for the drums, Mike's bass direct, and I put my amp in the middle room," he says, referring to the tape storage area between the control room and the rec room. "I didn't know where else to put it—I didn't want to overdub to the bass and drums; I wanted to play live.

So I stood in here, me and Mike played together, and my amp was in there. It's funny, because Valerie and everybody were in the rec room watching TV, and they couldn't hear anything but the guitar.

"I used a Fender 12-string on 'Cabo'—except for the solo, of course. There's a wah-wah on the solo—barely audible, though. I just used it for the sustain, not like Clapton wah-wah. I used the Bradshaw on 'Black & Blue.' I don't remember where else. I don't like a lot of jape—just a little bit of tasty echo to fill it out a little bit, sometimes a little Harmonizer. I mean, what else do you really need? What other effects are there? I'm not into effects, so I don't really even know what's out there. See, like all this stuff here," he says, pointing toward the built-in console, "is basically just different kinds of echoes and different kinds of doublings—that's it. I don't want no room simulator for my guitar! I got rooms."

Lets get back to *OU812*—or whatever the album will ultimately be called.

"This is the most unusual album we've done in terms of the way it was done," Ed says. "We wrote one song, put it down, wrote another one, put it down—we concentrated on one song at a time. Whereas with every other record, we'd put down all the basic tracks and then overdub. The first one I wrote was 'When It's Love.' I was so focused into that song that it took me a couple of days to think about another tune. Second one was 'Mine All Mine'—since I figured, 'Might as well get two keyboard tunes out of the way.' When I was writing that, I had to change gears, because 'When It's Love' was still in my head, and it took me a bit to shift. And then, I was so into 'Mine All Mine' that I totally forgot how to play 'When It's Love.' Understand what I'm saying? And that went on with every song, because we didn't do them all in a row. The only two that I had seeds of ideas for when we started were 'Naturally Wired' and 'Black & Blue.' Everything else was written as we went along—and basically I wrote pretty quickly. Like 'Cabo'—I wrote that in one day."

Did Sammy bring in any lyrics for Ed to write music to?

"No, he would get inspired by the music. Actually, Sammy wanted to write a song about Cabo. He had just come back from there and I had just written the music. And he said, 'This is perfect for Cabo!'

"You know," Ed reflects, "I haven't heard a rock and roll record like this in a long time. Maybe I'm just out of touch or something, but there's so many different things on it. I dunno. I guess I'm just real happy with it. I'm jazzed."

What are his choices for singles?

"To me, 'When It's Love' is just a classic tune," Ed replies, going down the list again. "It's pretty, it's heavy, it's melodic, it's sin-galong…it's just a happening song. Whereas 'Black & Blue' is heavy funk—it's slippery, it's grungy, more of a kids'…what am I talkin' about—I'm a kid. But I'd like the first single to be something grungi-er. I don't want people to think, 'Oh, Van Halen went pop.'

"There's only two songs on here that are keyboard-oriented. What I'm sayin' is, 'When It's Love' and 'Feel So Good' are very melodic songs, which people could consider pop and not Van Halen. Whereas 'Mine All Mine' is a keyboard tune, but it's smokin'. I dou-bled the keys with the guitar, and it sounds tripped-out. And 'Finish What You Started' will totally trip people out—it sounds like a cross between the Stones and us. It's probably the most atypical thing you'll ever hear from us—outside of 'Apolitical Blues.' When the Scorpions came up here, first thing we played them was 'Finish What You Started,' just to freak them out. They were sitting here going, 'Oh ja, ja. Ees very nice…' But they were looking at each oth-er like, 'Was that them?' And then my brother walked in and said, 'Hey, you guys are doing a great job pretending you like it.' " Ed breaks up with laughter at the recollection.

"I'll play anybody anything from this record," he says, "Because everything's such a different vibe. You hear 'Apolitical Blues' and you say, 'That's Van Halen?!' I go, 'Yeah—hey, man, there's more than one side to Van Halen.' "

Maybe even the critics will go for this one.

"Oh, fuck the critics. You can print that. It's nice if they like them; it's also nice if they don't. Because they don't buy them any-way—they get them for free."

Tell us about the rest of the tunes.

" 'Sucker' (or 'Sucker in a three-piece') is kind of like a 'Panama' beat. 'Source' is a major fast boogie—really cookin'. It's got a neat intro, too. Oh, you know what's got a real weird intro is 'Naturally Wired,' or whatever we're calling that one. It's hard to figure out where the beat is, because Al doesn't start out on the 'one.' It's actually a drum beat I came up with years ago, and Al said, 'Hey, man—this beat would be great for this one.' I don't know, it's probably something Zeppelin would have done. And then I come in with finger-tappin' stuff, and you can't figure out what's going on until we all come in, and you say, 'Oh, there's the beat.' Hey, and here's Donn!"

Landee walks into the control room, just two hours behind schedule—which is precisely in keeping with the way this album was made. "Hey, Donn, why don't you play some of the stuff for him?" I've just hit pay dirt. Van Halen exits, and Landee racks up a tape of completed mixes, cranks the master volume to 11, and lets 'er rip. In these circumstances, through the huge monitors, the music is nothing less than astounding, especially "When It's Love," a rock anthem if ever there was one; "Cabo," a slithering mass of inter-locked riffs and rhythms; "Finish What You Started," wherein Edward's fingerpicked direct Strat picks up where "Honky Tonk Women" left off; and "Feels So Good," an exhilarating marriage of buoyant keyboards and breakneck drumming. Alex is a monster throughout the album (Ed explained that his brother stopped drinking, which made a huge difference in his drum work), and Edward is nothing less than spectacular at simply being Edward. Wow.

As Landee plays the cuts, my tape recorder continues to roll—most likely overloading from the volume. When Ed returns and sees my machine recording, he instantly metamorphoses into Edward. "Hey, what's this?" he demands. Oops. "I'm making a bootleg," I deadpan. "Actually, I forgot to turn it off." Edward isn't buying it, but Ed reappears before things get gnarly. "Hey, you'll get your free CD soon enough," he jokes, before rewinding my tape to the top of the music and ensuring that the tunes will be overlayed by talk. Fair enough, Ed.

We get back into a listening mode, and Van Halen pushes my chair into the middle of the room so I'll get the full effect. He seems quite eager to get an honest reaction from the first outsider to hear this music. He repeatedly leans over and yells comments in my ear. During "When It's Love," he shouts, "Check this out—this solo is really different"; and, in the middle of the solo section: "Clapton. See, I still have some of that in me." While "Feels So Good" plays, he says, "Makes me want to dance—and I don't dance!" and launches into an impromptu Van Halen hip-hop.

You know something? This is fun. As a matter of fact, I'm beginning to notice a tingling sensation spreading over my entire body. Whaddaya know—this stuff is making my fur rise. I present my forearm to Ed for inspection.

"See?!" Ed/Eddie/Edward shouts triumphantly over the glorious sounds of a great band at its absolute zenith. "The chill factor. That's what rock and roll is all about—it's a feeling."

GUITAR WORLD, FEBRUARY 1990

THE MONSTER OF ROCK

He sparked an Eruption—and an aftershock of monumental proportions: Edward Van Halen, GUITAR WORLD's player of the decade.

By Joe Bosso

"**L**OOK AT THIS mess!" Eddie Van Halen takes in the barren and dusty confines of the apparent wreck and ruin of 5150, his beloved recording studio/clubhouse. Where most men find rest and rumination in neighborhood bars, Eddie has for years sought refuge in this, his hangout-joint to end all hangout-joints. Here he stays up late, pours back some Buds with his buds and plays his videos. Here, too, he cranks it to hell and back, capturing bits of genius on two-inch tape.

But at this moment he couldn't nail a solo banjo track in here, let alone the monstrous sonic booms for which Van Halen is universally celebrated. 5150 is being remodeled, so everything's been stripped away, sawed-off, gutted. Amps, effects racks, consoles—all gone. Construction will take at least a few months to complete, at which time the dream-like studio will sport a new look and house, for the first time, a drum room. But on this picture-perfect Hollywood day, poor Eddie Van Halen looks like a man without a country.

"What are you gonna do?" he shrugs, accompanying *Guitar World* Associate Publisher Greg Di Benedetto and I out onto the driveway. "That's where we're building the new house." He motions across the small valley that lies between the Van Halens' modest (by rock star and TV actress standards) one-bedroom digs and their soon-to-be constructed palatial estate. Half-a-dozen workmen are engaged in various digging, pouring and pounding activities. The house glistens in the L.A. sun and, while unfinished, looks like an architect's dream. Eddie grins a grin as only he can, lights a cigarette and assesses the situation with characteristic amusement. "The thing's taking twice as long as it was supposed to, and it's costing six times as much!"

EVH looks good: California-tanned, thinner than he's been in recent years and sturdy. He pads about the room, casually comfortable in beyond-baggy jeans, T-shirt and well-worn sneakers, with the cool, somewhat oblivious air peculiar to the mega-rich. For all that, it almost seems as if Eddie Van Halen is really just another guy, a bud—a dude. Perhaps that's how he likes it—as if the Porsches, Mercedes and Lamborghinis cluttering the driveway and parking lot could disappear tomorrow and it really wouldn't be that big a deal. Most successful rockers would take a journalist down to the wine cellar, but Eddie's idea of fun is showing off his motorized skateboard ("You can really clock yourself on the head when you fall off that thing at 35!"), or visiting his guitar room for a little stroll down memory lane.

"This place is a bit of a mess, too," he explains, running his hands along the bodies of guitar after guitar, as if to reacquaint himself with his collection of lovelies. "I don't usually keep 'em in cases because guitars are meant to be functional, you know?" [*Later in the day, as we prepared to drive into downtown L.A. for a photo shoot, Eddie took his famous Frankenstein striped Strat and his 5150 guitars, among others, and tossed the whole bunch in the back of his pickup truck like they were two-by-fours. As each guitar landed with a loud thud, I gave Eddie a somewhat astonished, quizzical look. He simply grinned. "I don't use cases for these either!"*]

"There's the Electro-Harmonix over there," he points to the keyboard just near the stairs. "I used that on 'Sunday Afternoon in the Park.' And there's the Destroyer I used to use," he says, pointing to one of the guitars hanging on the wall. "That was the one on *Women and Children First*. Oh, and here's what a VARIAC looks like!" Eddie's enthusiasm waxes as he holds up a harmless-looking electrical device that is most commonly used to dim wall lights. Eddie, of course, has for years routinely slapped them in his amps to better modify the voltage.

He ambles back outside where, plopped on a picnic table near the swimming pool, he reflects on a career that has not only brought him worldwide acclaim, fame and untold wealth, but, more important, has forever changed the way people play and listen to the electric guitar.

Although it is difficult today to imagine modern rock guitar without Eddie's influence, surprisingly, when the group that bears his surname released their debut album in early 1978, they were perceived as something of a throwback. While most popsters were caught up in the minimalism of post-punk, with its arty blend of end-of-the-world nihilism and Euro-style detachment, along came this louder-than-loud Southern California band of party-crazed Gypsies, blowing up amps and pillaging any unsuspecting town in their path. Their equipment was crude and their songs were empty-headed supplications to the pleasures of limitless wine, women and song. At a time when Gary Numan and Kraftwerk were setting the trends and the electric guitar was taking a back seat to the synthesizer, it appeared that this band didn't stand a chance.

Enter the round-cheeked Eddie Van Halen. As fast as he could unleash a flurry of dizzying harmonics, he tapped his way into our hearts, the first to infuse the electric guitar with genuinely new blood since Jimi Hendrix. For even if the young Van Halen's recording career had ended the moment he unplugged after tracking the seminal solo tour de force "Eruption," his place in the history of the electric guitar would have been assured. With this much-imitated instrumental, Van Halen single-handedly introduced the hammer-on to a generation of guitarists. Not only did "Eruption" serve to usher in an important, unconventional artist, it signaled the rise of something greater than that—it launched a movement. Overnight, the stakes were forever altered—and guitarists worldwide knew it seconds after their needles hit Van Halen vinyl.

In 1982 Eddie, by then an established rock star (a term he despises), received a call from producer Quincy Jones, who was working on a red-hot rock and roll track for a Michael Jackson album. Would Eddie come to the studio and lay down a solo? Sure, thought Eddie, why not? Might be fun. David Lee Roth had always frowned upon the idea of Eddie playing on other people's records, but hey, this was a Michael Jackson record, so Van Halen fans certainly wouldn't be interested—probably wouldn't even hear it. Eddie grabbed his guitar and split for the studio. Once there, he found that he liked what he heard, the driving song called "Beat It." The track was pretty much all there; Steve Lukather had recorded most of the guitars, and all that was needed was a solo—a hot one, to really make the tune cook.

After making the crucial suggestion that he solo over the verse section rather than the breakdown, as was originally planned, Eddie winged it. The solo would turn out to be Eddie's most popular and most analyzed work of the Eighties. All fired up, whooping and swirling, growling and shrieking, it is the product of a heart meeting a mind and connecting with the unknown.

It's a head-turner all right, and for more than the obvious reasons. Eddie Van Halen was the perfect choice to play the solo, and his cameo spot in a Michael Jackson song carried repercussions that went far beyond guitar heroics. Until then MTV, still in its infancy, had maintained an unwritten rule against the airing of "black"-oriented videos. Although the network somewhat reluctantly agreed to air Jackson's "Billie Jean," it was a hollow victory, a response borne more out of record company pressure than popular opinion. But Eddie's star-turn on "Beat It" demolished the color barrier with stunning, decisive force. MTV had to respond. And it didn't end there. Suddenly, FM hard rock stations, which primarily catered to white suburbanites, were deluged with calls for "Beat It." Across the country, white males, who ordinarily would never dream of buying a Michael Jackson album, were doing so in record numbers. At the same time, black stations—the last places one would expect to hear searing, burning, heavy metal guitar—were wearing out their copies of "Beat It."

It seemed appropriate that Van Halen's brilliant and influential solo was the product of a whim. For this artist is—musically and personally—the personification of explosive spontaneity.

Eddie sits back in his chair, lights another cigarette and grins that grin. The greatest guitarist in the world is ready to talk about 10 incredible years gone by.

GUITAR WORLD: What is the single thing you're most proud of having accomplished in the last decade?

VAN HALEN: I guess it's that I introduced and came out with a slightly different style, and that a lot of people have picked up on it.

GW: The song "Eruption" changed everything practically overnight.

VAN HALEN: Well, that's kind of what I'm saying, that I changed the way people played the guitar, you know? I mean, you see everybody doing it, and they weren't until I did it. So it's kind of obvious. It's not like I'm on an ego trip or anything.

GW: What's your take on the L.A. band scene nowadays? How has it changed since you played the clubs?

VAN HALEN: I think, in a funny way, that Van Halen kind of paved the way for that, too. When we were playing the clubs, there was no room for a bunch of long-haired, platformed, goofy-lookin' fools! [*laughs*] It was real hard for us to get into the clubs. It was always [*in gruff voice*], "You're too loud, your guitar's too psychedelic, etc." We used to get fired because you'd have to play five sets of Top 40 stuff, and we'd only have one set—which we'd play for the audition. We'd get the gig, play our one set of Top 40 songs, and then start playing our own stuff. Halfway through the second set the club owner would be screaming, "Hey! Get the hell outta here!" So we'd have to start playing our own gigs.

GW: A lot of bands do that nowadays—the self-promotion thing.

VAN HALEN: I'm not really too familiar with the club scene today. I don't even know where to go if I want to go to a club. I don't get out much.

GW: There's the pay-for-play thing happening.

VAN HALEN: Like at [*Los Angeles club*] Gazarri's? I heard about that. You have to pay to play?

GW: Bands have to pay something like $1500 to play.

VAN HALEN: I'll tell you, making 75 bucks a night isn't much better! [*laughs*] It sure isn't enough to buy equipment. I mean, Alex and I used to go around and paint house numbers on curbs to make extra money.

GW: Who are some of the players that have impressed you during the past decade?

VAN HALEN: Well, there's Satriani and Vai. They're excellent players. [*pauses*] I don't really listen to anything! I'm always wrapped up doing my own stuff, always writing.

GW: Any lesser-known players?

VAN HALEN: Well, there's this band I'm producing called Private Life. And Danny Johnson, I love the way he plays. He's got that Louisiana blues sound, but he can also have the fire of Allan Holdsworth. He's got the vibe I really like.

GW: One of the things you pioneered was two-handed tapping.

VAN HALEN: I don't know if I was the first one to do it. I mean, I'm sure that somebody else thought of it, too! [*laughs*]

GW: Nevertheless, people equate Van Halen with pyrotechnics. You brought it to the masses.

VAN HALEN: Right. Funny thing is, I think I've mellowed out in my old age. I see a lot of people using it as a trick, but to me, it's just the way I play. It's not like, "Oh, oh, I'm gonna do a trick now!" I mean, you see these other guys playing and it's, "Watch this!" A trick. Like a vibrato bar—I don't use it as a trick, but as a way to play. I think I've gotten a little tastier through the years. I don't play as reckless-ly; I'm a little more melodic. I guess I'm much more into songs and songwriting.

GW: Does it bother you that people have focused so much on the two-handed tapping technique? That maybe some other aspects of your playing have been overlooked?

VAN HALEN: Yeah. I mean, whether I tap or not, I'm still a good player. If that's all I'm known for, then goddamn…

GW: There are so many technicians around now, people who can really wail. But there are very few sonic innovators—people whose sound is instantly recognizable.

VAN HALEN: I think that comes with time. When I first started playing, I was like—"brrrrrrrrr!"—as fast as I could go, too. It was fun. But as you mature a little bit, you see there's no point to it, and you start using your technique to bring out your style .

GW: When did you notice that you were progressing on the guitar a little faster than your peers? When did the term "guitar hero" begin to be tossed in your direction?

VAN HALEN: Probably when our first album came out.

GW: But before then, there must have been people who said you were a pretty hot player.

VAN HALEN: Well, yeah, when other people tell you, sure. Okay!

GW: You've always acknowledged the mistakes on Van Halen albums. What are some of the most amusing examples?

VAN HALEN: All kinds of stuff! I don't think there's any one song of ours that's done right all the way through. [*laughs*] Sometimes I'm out of tune a little bit. I heard "Where Have All the Good Times Gone?" on the radio the other day, and I'm doing these harmonics…missed 'em. I kinda chuckled.

GW: But most people would've removed their mistakes.

VAN HALEN: Especially nowadays. Everything's so technically advanced. I'm not really a perfectionist, in that sense. I'm more for a vibe.

GW: There was a pretty good goof in your cover of "Pretty Woman." You forgot part of the bridge.

VAN HALEN: Yeah. I screwed up! [*laughs*] I never bought the record, I didn't know how the song went, so it was, "I think this is how it goes," you know? And so we did it, and realized later that it was wrong. I met Roy Orbison at Farm Aid. I don't even know if he knew we did it. You know, everybody was pushing for cover tunes on *Diver Down*, so I said, "Well, let's at least do 'Pretty Woman'"—it's got a riff, unlike some of the other stuff we were doing.

GW: Did you intend to go right from "Intruder" into "Pretty Woman"?

VAN HALEN: Oh, that was an afterthought. We'd done the video for "Pretty Woman" and needed something else for it, so we went in the studio and just tagged that on. I was drinking a beer—that's me sliding the can on the strings—"A-rooo! A-rooo!"

GW: Van Halen's sound on your first couple of records was very much that of a raw, live band. But this has changed somewhat. Now it's a fuller, more produced sound.

VAN HALEN: Yeah, well, the main thing in the beginning was that I had never been in the studio before. I remember asking Ted Templeman and Don Landee, "Hey, do you mind if I just play like I do live?" Because I didn't have any rhythm parts underneath the solos. I didn't know how to overdub. That's why it sounds live—it is!

GW: What noticeable changes have you made in the way you now lay down basic tracks?

VAN HALEN: See, a lot of times I'll still do a live solo, but I'll just overdub the rhythm part underneath. I guess we're just getting better at recording. The technology has advanced so much since '77!

GW: Do you think your guitar sound has changed any?

VAN HALEN: Believe it or not, I'm using the exact same stuff I always have. I have an old baby Marshall. And Kramers, which I started playing about five or six years ago. I don't know, I just turn everything all the way up! I used to use those old MXR Phase 90s on all the solos—it's kind of a cool sound. I don't use that much now, though. I have a rack that looks like computer shit, but I don't even know what's on it. [*pauses*] The only thing I use is a little bit of delay and a couple of Harmonizers. It's not a real tight echo.

GW: You've been successful for some years now. How do you fend off complacency, the whole "rock star" trip?

VAN HALEN: See, all I do is make music. I don't go out. I just sit up here on the hill, in my studio. I've always been that way, so nothing's different. A lot of people want to be successful so they can go out and party and have fun. But to me, making music is the fun part. I'm a weirdo! [*laughs*] I mean, that's what you saw out there [*points in the direction of the studio*].

GW: "Beat It" created such a buzz. How did your involvement with that song come about?

VAN HALEN: Quincy Jones called me up to ask if I wanted to play on Michael Jackson's record.

GW: Of course, at the time, Michael Jackson wasn't the pop icon that he is today.

VAN HALEN: I didn't think he was. But when that record came out, it sure was a big one! It was really funny. I was out back, and something was wrong with the phone. And you know, there's always people calling me. So I said, "Hello?" And there was this guy answering, "Hello?" We couldn't hear each other, so I hung up. And then the call came again: "Is this Eddie? It's Quincy, man!" And I'm like, "Who the hell? What do you want, you asshole?" [*laughs*] So finally he says, "It's Quincy Jones, man!" And I'm thinking, "Oh shit— I'm sorry, man." It was really funny. After the record, he wrote me a letter thanking me, signed, "The Asshole." [*laughs*]

GW: Did you work the solo out before you cut it?

VAN HALEN: No, I just noodled along. I actually changed part of the song, though, because they wanted me to solo over the break. So I said, "Can we edit it to a verse, so there's some chord changes?" Then I just soloed over what I thought should be the solo section. I did two solos, and they picked the one they liked. That was it. It took about 20 minutes to do. And there was Michael, standing in the back saying [*mimics Michael Jackson*] "I really like that high fast stuff you do!" [*laughs*]

GW: It seemed logical to assume that as of result of "Beat It" you'd receive a lot of offers to play on other people's records. Yet we haven't seen you do much of that.

VAN HALEN: Yeah, well, just recently Stevie Nicks...Steve Perg...everybody's calling. Thank God I have an answering machine! [*laughs*] Believe it or not, I did the Michael Jackson thing because I figured nobody'd know. I swear to God. The band—Roth, my brother and

Mike—always hated me doing things outside of Van Halen. They'd say, "Keep it in the band." And it just so happened that Roth was on one of his Amazon jungle trips or whatever he does, and Al was out of town, and Mike was out at Disneyland or something, so I couldn't consult them. So I just said, "Damn it, I'll do it and no one will ever know." So then it comes out and becomes song of the year and everything. My brother still won't let me live it down. And I did it for free, too! [laughs]

GW: What about Tone Loc sampling "Jamie's Cryin'"?

VAN HALEN: [Excitedly] Oh, right! I'm sitting around watching MTV one day and I think, "That sure sounds like my guitar and Al's drums..."

GW: Wait a second. The story I had from the label is that you were consulted.

VAN HALEN: Hell, no! I was just sitting there, and I hear my brother's drums. And then there's my guitar! So I called up our manager and said, "What is this shit?" So I guess he called them up and said that they should at least thank us. [laughs] And I guess we're thanked on the record.

GW: This is done all the time these days. A lot of rap uses hard rock and heavy metal guitar samples.

VAN HALEN: I think it's a bullshit thing. I mean, why don't they just have someone else play it? It's kinda thin, you know?

GW: Let me ask you about your hearing. Does Pete Townshend's problem cause you any concern?

VAN HALEN: Well, I'll tell you one thing I don't do, and that's stack my cabinets. Even in the old days, when I used to have the mountainous shit, I only used the bottom cabinets. Just don't stand in front of the stuff. I like to stand in front of them so I can feel my arm hairs move—but not the hair on my head.

GW: You mentioned Satriani and Vai earlier, but did anybody else who came up during the Eighties make you sweat—maybe just a little?

VAN HALEN: No. See, nobody makes me sweat. If anything, when I hear somebody good, it inspires me, you know? Like when I first heard Holdsworth, that made me want to play! To me, music isn't a competitive thing. There are so many good players around—I'm not in competition with them. I'm not out to be better than anybody. Music is such a personal thing. How can you say someone's better than someone else?

GW: Well, there is some lame stuff out there.

VAN HALEN: [*Explodes with laughter*] That's true!

GW: You were pretty involved with Holdsworth's career for a while there.

VAN HALEN: Yeah, I got him signed to Warner Bros. because I just hated to see this guy who's so amazing selling guitars to stay alive. So I got him signed. I was supposed to co-produce the record with Ted Templeman and Donn Landee. Then—I hate to say this—while we were on tour in South America he just didn't wanna wait like two weeks, you know? So he did it himself...and it ended up being just another Allan Holdsworth record. The guy needs direction, you know what I mean? We did a couple of demos before I went to South America, and one of the songs was great. So he blew it, I think. I really think I could have, well, not necessarily pulled him back, but steered him in a different direction, you know? I was just over my friend Steve Lukather's house, and he played me Allan's new record, and I tell you, I couldn't tell the difference between that and his other records. I don't wanna rag on the guy, because he's an incredible player and he's a good friend. I love him. He just needs direction, that's all.

GW: Have you worked with him since that episode?

VAN HALEN: Yeah, I talked to him on the phone about a month ago. He called and asked if I'd want to do something with him. And I'd love to, except I don't really have the time right now. When the time is right, sure. It'll be fun. I don't give a damn if it's good or not. Like that thing I did with Brian May; that wasn't good, but it was fun.

I'd sure like to see how Holdsworth does some of his stuff, but I never had the nerve to ask him. It takes me two hands to do what he does with one. I don't know how he pulls it off! I mean, I have a hell of a reach, too, you know? I'd also love to pick Jimmy Page's brain about how he got some of those sounds. It'd be more in terms of sounds than, "How'd you play this?"

GW: How do you feel about Page these days? He's been getting a bad rap.

VAN HALEN: And that's bullshit. He's a genius. He's a great player, a songwriter and producer, so there you go. Put it this way: He might not be the greatest executor or whatever, but when you hear a Page solo, he speaks. I've always said that Clapton was my main influence, but Page was actually more the way I am, in a reckless abandon kind of way.

GW: Do you still tinker around, building guitars, as you used to?

VAN HALEN: Not as much as I used to. The only reason I did that was because I was trying to find—well, not necessarily the perfect guitar, but the guitar that served my means. I'll show you... [*Eddie exits, returning momentarily with his famous striped Strat with the Kramer neck.*] It does exactly what I want it to do. I used to build guitars because I wanted one that had a Gibson sound, but with a vibrato bar. I wanted a Strat with a Gibson sound, and that's what this is.

GW: A lot of guitar manufacturers have taken cues from you over the years.

VAN HALEN: Oh, God, tell me about it.

GW: The non-pickguard. You were about the first to...

VAN HALEN: The whole vibrato bar, one-pickup thing was my idea. It was actually a mistake, the way I came up with it. I bought a Strat, and took a chisel to it to carve out the rear pickup cavity, the one by the bridge, so I could drop a humbucker into it . But as I removed the pickguard and put the new pickup in, I didn't know how to re-wire it—you know, I couldn't get the wires back in. So I thought, "Wow, I wonder how it'll work just straight to the volume knob." So I left it like that. Then I made myself a plastic pickguard to cover up the holes, and that's how this concept was born. You know, when I used to play Les Pauls I could never get a good sound out of the front and rear pickups at the same time. If you get a nice fat sound out of the back one and then you put it on the front, it's real muddy. Either that or you have to set it so bright to get a good sound out of the front one that the back pickup sounds like shit. So I just said, "Damn, what do I need two pickups for?"

GW: You don't strike me as a real EQ freak or anything.

VAN HALEN: Oh, no. I just turn everything up! [*laughs*]

GW: If you turn everything up with some Marshalls, there's either too much treble or too much bass.

VAN HALEN: Yeah, that's why I use the old ones. Any time I see an old one, I buy it. Even if it sounds like shit, because they can be made to sound good.

GW: Is the VARIAC still a part of your sound?

VAN HALEN: Yep.

GW: Does that actually change the voltage?

VAN HALEN: Yeah, that's all it does.

GW: And you plug the output of the amplifier into the VARIAC?

VAN HALEN: Yeah. That's all. It's a light dimmer! I use a studio light dimmer. See, it enables you to play at a lower volume, but you can still get the balls of the amp. I blew out the house once, when we used to live in this little shack in Pasadena. We had this little light dimmer in the wall, and I thought, "Wow, I wonder what'll happen if I hook my amp up to that?" [*This is a dangerous procedure and should not, under any circumstances, be attempted.—GW Ed.*]

GW: Once the VARIAC is installed, you just lower the dimmer and run the amp up full—it acts like a master volume control, and does so without your having to lower the master volume control on the amp.

VAN HALEN: And you get the whole output of the amp. Know what I mean? It sounds sweet.

GW: What do you think of the guitar sounds we're hearing today? What do you think when you turn on the radio?

VAN HALEN: I think everybody sounds the same. Playing-wise, too. Everybody has a Marshall stack now, and a guitar like this [*holds up his guitar*] or a Les Paul. Nobody's doing anything different. It all sounds like razor blades coming at your ears after a while. Just fuzzed out noise.

GW: What if you were a kid today, and there's already an Edward Van

Halen out there. What would you do to avoid sounding like a carbon copy?

VAN HALEN: I don't know…maybe pull out some old Cream records. Listen to old blues stuff and get your feel happening, instead of just jumpin' in and playing as fast as you can, copying the latest hit on the radio. I mean, I don't know what scales are—I just play what sounds right to me. I never had a lesson in my life. So, this scale or that scale, I don't know. To me, you have 12 notes to work with, and whatever configuration you use is up to you.

GW: But didn't you study music theory as a kid?

VAN HALEN: I was supposed to. It takes too long to learn. I don't even like to read books! If I had to learn to read music, it would take forever.

GW: So a certain amount of ignorance is bliss?

VAN HALEN: I think the grass is green on both sides—as long as you don't get too caught up in that reading-the-chart syndrome.

GW: What about someone like U2's The Edge, who doesn't have a whole lot of chops but still created an identifiable sound.

VAN HALEN: He sure likes his echo, doesn't he? But see, there again, he's more of a songwriter, and that's where it's at. Expressing yourself in a song is a lot more wide open then. All these kids who are just gunslingers, they'll come around. You can't be doing that all your life—it's impossible.

GW: Do you ever feel, in a very small way, responsible for the emphasis on speed-playing today?

VAN HALEN: For kids playing like typewriters? Hey, that's not my fault! Maybe they cop the speed because they can't cop my feel. Maybe they shouldn't think so much. I don't think when I play. I get the basic parts of the song and then, when I start soloing, I don't think.

GW: While we're on the subject of sound, "Finish What You Started" is kind of a departure for you.

VAN HALEN: It's a direct Strat. It was just for fun. We actually set out and tried to do something different, something goofy, and it worked.

GW: Is it too early to talk about what you might do on the next Van

Halen record?

VAN HALEN: Oooh. [*pauses*] Anything and everything. Sammy and I are already writing, and we're comin' up with some really neat shit.

GW: Is there any format you follow when you write together?

VAN HALEN: Uh, I come up with music, he calls me and comes up with a concept, an idea—God, I don't wanna give anything away here—and he'll inspire me to write something. And then when I do, I'll inspire him, in turn, to write the lyrics to it. And then we sit down together and work it out. Then Al and Mike jump in and say, "We don't like that!" [*laughs*] No, I'm kidding. We never really write in the studio. The studio's just where we go to record. I just sit around with my guitar and a little cassette machine.

We've never had the luxury to do what we're doing right now, and that is stockpiling a bunch of tunes and then when we're ready to put it out, putting it out. Because with *5150*, you know, everybody was wondering what was going on with Van Halen, so we released it. And with *OU812*, we were already committed to do the Monsters of Rock before the record was even done. We would have preferred to finish the record, put it out, waited a bit, made sure we liked the record, and then booked a tour. That's what we're going to do this time.

GW: How do you feel today about the Monsters of Rock tour?

VAN HALEN: A lot of people slammed us for it, but we sold a lot of tickets. Not all of them were sold out, but hey, they were stadiums. That same year, Aerosmith and Guns N' Roses did the same thing, and they only sold like 30,000 seats outdoors. I didn't hear anybody raggin' about that.

GW: You received so much flack about playing keyboards. Do you think people still don't see you as a keyboard player?

VAN HALEN: I love playing keyboards, man. I write a lot of stuff on keys. It's like they don't want to realize that I play keyboards. See, here's the thing: When Dave was in the band, he would say, "Hey, man, nobody wants to see you play keyboards!" And I felt like, "If I wanna play keyboards or if I wanna play tuba, I'll play it."

GW: Are you as much a tinkerer with keyboards as you are with the guitar?

VAN HALEN: Nah. I just like fooling around with sounds. I love the old OB-8s because they're hands-on, you know? You can just turn a knob and change the sound. You don't have to be a computer whiz. Nice, thick sound too; I think they sound better than the digital stuff.

GW: People associate you so much with note-heavy solos, but your solo in "Dreams" is surprising: For roughly half the solo you only play two notes.

VAN HALEN: Yeah. It just felt right. When I'm behind the console, overdubbing, I just say, "Hmmm, let's try this." If that doesn't work, I'll try something else. Sometimes I get a solo right off, and other times I'll be doing it all afternoon and…nothing.

GW: Do you have much of a problem with writer's block?

VAN HALEN: Sure, don't you? Sometimes things just don't come. So I just walk away from it. Actually, sometimes, I'll try and work through it. I'll get pissed off and think, "I gotta beat this thing!" But other times it doesn't work. There are no rules. Sometimes it can happen for you, sometimes not. Put it this way—if you're up for 24 hours and getting nowhere, it's time to call it quits.

GW: Van Halen has, of late, enjoyed a good relationship with the rock press. But up until *1984*, it seemed like you guys couldn't do anything to get a good review.

VAN HALEN: I think they just realized that we're here to stay, you know? It's like a roach that won't go away. Finally it's, "Okay, stay!" It used to bother me, because some of these guys didn't know what they were talking about. If you don't like what someone does, then say you don't like it—but don't say it stinks. I mean, who are they to say something isn't good? At least say that you just don't like it as a personal preference, an opinion.

GW: One thing rarely pointed out is the band's ability to sing some wonderful background vocals. Does that bug you?

VAN HALEN: That's a unique part of the Van Halen sound. That's Michael and me. I don't really care if people comment or not. That's just the way we are, that's part of the sound.

GW: A lot of bands just can't sing.

VAN HALEN: It's true ! The thing is, I'm not a singer, but I can hit a note. I have good pitch. Endurance is tough. Two beers, three songs, and I'm out.

GW: Do you think Michael Anthony has gotten short shrift from the press?

VAN HALEN: Sure. Because he's not a showboat kind of guy. Part of the reason I stick out so much is that Mike doesn't steal the show. I mean, if he wanted to hog the show, so to speak, we'd be butting heads. And if we tried to do unison things, what would be the point? I like the guys on the three instruments to be playing their own thing; I don't want everybody doing things together. The counterpoint thing, that's what I like. Just like the old Cream jams: They were all in their own worlds, but it worked.

GW: Let's look ahead 10 years. Do you see yourself doing the same thing, with the same band?

VAN HALEN: Oh, yeah. Definitely. I'm totally into family, so to speak. There's no reason why I can't be doing the same thing. I just want to make music and have fun. As long as you have the fire and you still want to do it, fine. When it starts getting old to me, then I'll start doing something else. I don't know what—maybe a race car driver!

Ebet Roberts

GUITAR WORLD, SEPTEMBER 1991

LORD OF THE STRINGS

With his spanking Ernie Ball guitar and Peavey amp in hand, Van Halen struck a blow FOR UNLAWFUL CARNAL KNOWLEDGE.

By Brad Tolinski

"TURN LEFT! WATCH that curve!" Associate Publisher Greg Di Benedetto can't contain his annoyance at my feeble attempts to navigate the treacherous mountain road that leads to 5150, Edward Van Halen's legendary home studio in Los Angeles. "You idiot," hisses Di Benedetto. "Pay attention to the damn signs! You fool, don't you know what happens to New Yorkers who lose their way in the vicious outback of Hollywood Hills? Buzzard bait!"

My first instinct is to reprimand the man for his sharp-tongued babble. But his frenzied expression makes me think twice. It's not good policy to mess with a serious Van Halen zealot—particularly when barreling down the Baja at 87 m.p.h. in a unstable Galaxy 500. The rabid bastard will probably rip my lungs out.

" 'Errruption!' 'ICE CREAM MAN!' " roars my twisted compatriot. I seize the exclusive map of "L.A.'s 10 Holiest Sites," presented to me by the people at Tanquery Liquor, and search for Van Halen's 5150 studio. To my consternation, I discover that this greatest of shrines has somehow been excluded. I conclude that the directory is probably the work of silly misfits and drunkards, and toss the offensive booklet out the window in disgust.

Suddenly, my companion points and bellows like a walrus hit by a stun gun. I jam the brakes and receive a mouthful of gritty road dust for my pains. By divine providence, we have miraculously stumbled upon the entrance to Eddie's rambling estate. Di Benedetto gasps, awe-struck: "Eldorado!"

We chug up a small hill, past Ed and wife Valerie Bertinelli's palatial Tudor-style house, and pull into a deserted driveway situated in front of a small, hut-like building: 5150. Di Benedetto and I leap from the car and gaze reverently upon the birthplace of "Hot for Teacher."

5150 is hardly the last word in opulence; the newly expanded studio looks rather bland—something like a large tool shed. But no one feels let down. We are, after all, standing in the presence of the temple of distortion, the grand mosque of two-handed tapping and devastatingly heavy squealing. Maureen O'Connor, Van Halen's super-efficient publicist, appears and leads us inside. You can tell Maureen's a pro—she politely pretends not to notice my partner's imbecile grin, and responds with stoical forbearance when he stubbornly insists on singing a brief hymn as we enter the studio.

As we explore 5150's dim interior, Di Benedetto roughly squeezes my shoulder when he spies the king's ancient Marshall. Flanking the legendary 100-watt head are two of Edward's recent acquisitions: a purple Soldano and a new, prototype 5150 Peavey head. We are dismayed that he would use anything other than his Super Lead, but who are we to question the ways of Ed? Van Halen, we whisper in agreement, works in mysterious ways.

Unfortunately, there is little time to gawk, and we are quickly hustled to a privileged spot behind the band's new API recording console. Maureen places a tape of *For Unlawful Carnal Knowledge* into a DAT machine and pumps the volume up to vicious, cornea-popping levels.

Producer/engineer Andy Johns [*Led Zeppelin, Rolling Stones*] and producer Ted Templeman [*David Lee Roth-era Van Halen, Doobie Brothers*] have done a hell of a job in capturing the band's explosive rhythm section. Alex Van Halen gives the performance of his life, tossing off a bizarre array of tom fills with deadly precision. And the grievously underrated bassist, Michael Anthony, is finally riding high in the mix. But the biggest surprise is Edward's brutish, guitar-army approach on tracks like "Pleasure Dome," "Spanked" and the single, "Poundcake."

At the tape's conclusion we are escorted to the studio's lounge.

"Hey, man!" says an energetic figure sporting red Converse sneakers and a huge grin. Edward Van Halen hops over and enthusiastically shakes our hands, oblivious to our disheveled condition—and gaping mouths. "Howzit goin'?"

Van Halen unpretentiously settles into a battered antique barber's chair, takes a drag on his cigarette, and quietly asks what it is that *Guitar World* wants to know.

GUITAR WORLD: This is the dawn of a new era for you. You've just released a new album, co-created a new guitar and worked with a new producer in a revamped studio. Was this part of some grand design?

EDWARD VAN HALEN: Believe it or not, no. We started our last tour in 1988 and ended it in Japan in February of 1989. We consciously took a whole year off, during which I barely touched the guitar. We saw each other socially, but we didn't do any work. Then in the early part of last year, we sat together and discussed what we wanted to accomplish, and everything just started falling into place. I don't want to spoil anybody's fantasies, but we rarely calculate anything. In general, we don't think that much.

GW: What was the first order of business?

VAN HALEN: Finding a producer. The name of Andy Johns, who produced most of Led Zeppelin's records, came up. Coincidentally, I had just met him in a recording studio while I was finishing production on the latest *Private Life* album. So we auditioned him.

GW: You auditioned Andy? He's worked on some of rock's greatest albums.

VAN HALEN: We needed to know whether we would get along with him on a personal level. Also, we wanted to see how he worked in the studio. All we knew was that he's made some great records. So we called him exactly one year ago today. He answered his phone and said [*assumes a growling, pub-drenched English accent*], "Hey mate, what do you want me to do? Come in and mess around a bit? No problem, but it's my birthday and I'm kind of hammered. Call me back tomorrow." He sounded like Dudley Moore in *Arthur*. And as it turned out, Andy is so rock and roll it's ridiculous. He really fit in.

GW: What did Andy's audition consist of?

VAN HALEN: We asked him to come around. At first he insisted on a second engineer, but we had to nix that idea because the studio is so small. So he came by himself. We started miking up the drums, and by the end of the day we were convinced that he was our man. He took control without being obnoxious.

GW: Did you have any music prepared at that point?

VAN HALEN: Absolutely nothing. That was the next big problem. [*laughs*] I wasn't really prepared, because I thought it would take a while to find someone we wanted to work with. The guys were asking me, "Hey Ed, you got any licks?" A little panicky, I said, "Hell no! Give me...uh...give me until tomorrow."

The first thing I came up with was a real headbanger called "Judgment Day." It's a pretty simple tune. I figured, "Gee, I haven't played guitar in a year, I can make it through this!" [*laughs*] After that song was finished we continued to jam in the studio, and slowly the tracks started to materialize.

The whole record was done one song at a time. We'd completely finish one track before moving on to the next one. That's why there are so many different textures on this record. It wasn't done like our first album, where we banged all the rhythm tracks out in a couple of days. Interestingly, I think this is a much more powerful rock and roll record than our last two, despite the fact that it was conceived over a long period of time.

GW: What did Andy bring to the record?

VAN HALEN: He brought rock and roll inspiration. More importantly, he is the first engineer to capture the sound of Van Halen's rhythm section. The bottom line is: If Al is happy, then I'm happy. It isn't hard to get a great guitar sound. It's much harder to get a fantastic acoustic drum sound—which I think Andy did.

GW: What modifications did you make in the studio?

VAN HALEN: We installed a new, warm-sounding API console, which was custom-fitted for our relatively small room. It's got 36 inputs and features GML automation, which made it much easier to mix. We also added a drum room that practically doubled the size of the studio. The additional room really helped Alex capture the sound he always wanted. In the past we had to resort to Simmons drums because there was no way to isolate an acoustic kit when we wanted to play together—there just wasn't enough room. Playing together without having to compromise our sound was a dream come true.

We really took our time on the actual recording process, and made sure each one of us was happy with the sound of our instruments. In a way, it's the ideal Van Halen record.

GW: Did Andy make suggestions regarding the arrangements?

VAN HALEN: Not really. Wait, let me rephrase that. What I really appreciated about Andy is that he gave me space when I needed to develop an idea.

GW: Why didn't you use engineer Donn Landee this time?

VAN HALEN: We weren't unhappy with Donn, but we've done eight records with him and felt it would be nice to get a different spin on things. It wasn't any big deal.

GW: What was Ted Templeman's role on this record?

VAN HALEN: Ted came in to save the day last January. We thought we should try to finish the record. Since none of us are very good at finishing things, we thought of Ted. He is—and if you read this, Ted, please don't take it the wrong way—a very organized cat. I mean, you put Andy Johns, Sammy Hagar, Alex Van Halen and Mike Anthony and me in a room together, and we'll piss up a rope for years, just having fun and experimenting. Ted finally said, "Enough is enough. What do you want, a double record? You'll be here for another year. Let's finish what we've got." He cracked the whip and pulled everything together. He also worked on a lot of the vocals with Sammy, while Andy and I worked on guitars and guitar overdubs.

GW: There are a lot of overdubs on this record, which is somewhat unusual for you. "Poundcake," for example, features a complete wall of sound.

VAN HALEN: It wasn't really planned, it's just the way everything evolved. I came up with a riff that didn't really excite anyone until Andy suggested I use some electric 12-strings to flesh out the rhythm tracks. It turned out to be just the thing the song needed. All of a sudden, the lyrics, the title, everything came into sharp focus. What you hear are two electric 12-strings doubled under my usual dirty guitar.

Earlier, you asked what Andy Johns brought to this record. That was it—the inspiration that comes from the sound element. He would make a small suggestion, or move a knob or two, and our sound would change, automatically goosing our creative juices.

GW: What kind of 12-string did you use?

VAN HALEN: It's a guitar developed by Roger Giffin, who works out of Gibson's custom shop. We worked together on my Steinberger guitars. His custom-12 has these small Smith pickups that look like something between a single-coil and a humbucker.

GW: On the solo in "Poundcake" it sounds like you were using your new neck pickup.

VAN HALEN: You're right. It was like, "All right! I've got a new toy!" The neck pickup is all over this record.

GW: It also sounds like you dug your old wah-wah out of the closet. You use it quite a bit.

VAN HALEN: People always ask me what I was thinking. I wasn't thinking! It was pretty spontaneous. A wah-wah happened to be floating around the studio, I plugged it in, and that was that. And I think that because it was handy, I used it on several tracks.

GW: You function on a very intuitive level, just by letting things flow.

VAN HALEN: Whenever I try to plan something, it never seems to work out. So why plan? It only seems to lead to disappointment.

GW: You've owned 5150 for quite a while now, and it's just a stone's throw from your house. I imagine that you tinker around. Have you grown more studio-sophisticated?

VAN HALEN: I know how to run the shit, believe it or not. Actually, this is kind of a touchy subject. In the old days Donn Landee kind of monopolized 5150. He was the only one who really knew how to run anything. It was his gig, so he was very protective and didn't want anyone else touching the knobs. Andy is just the opposite. He showed me how to run the console and seemed more than happy to receive my input. It was a real relief to finally know my way around, because I could go in and record ideas at any given time. I actually got to the point where I could punch myself in with my toes! I think my wife also punched me in on a couple of things. It was like, "Honey, when I count to four, push record!" My recording setup is so simple—you know, two Shure SM-57s on a Marshall cabinet—that it really wasn't any big deal.

GW: How do you mike your cabinet?

VAN HALEN: Two mics on the same speaker—one directly in the middle and one angled from the side.

GW: Why the angled microphone?

VAN HALEN: At one point Andy complained that he wasn't hearing enough bottom. So I said, "Okay, okay, then put another mic on the speaker." That's the way we solve problems in the studio. A lot of it is just common sense.

GW: This record is probably the most sonically varied and adventurous of your career. "Spanked" epitomizes this new experimental approach.

VAN HALEN: Again, it's totally unconscious. I didn't set out to make this an experimental record. For example, the guitar-like bass line on "Spanked" is a total fluke. One day Andy walked in with a Danelectro six-string bass, and I thought, "Oooh, that's neat." I plugged it into my Marshall and it sounded wild. It just seemed appropriate for the main lick in "Spanked."

GW: But it seems to me that if you're using a new guitar and are in the process of developing a new amp, at some point you must have consciously wanted to experiment with new sounds.

VAN HALEN: I'm not after a different sound; I'm just trying to find the epitome of what I've always heard in my head. Initially, the only reason I co-designed the new guitar was that Sterling Ball had been hounding me to do it for over a year. He was after my ass! Fender wanted me, too. At one point, all these guitar companies came out of the woodwork because I wasn't working with Kramer anymore. I went with Sterling because his company did a fine job with my 5150 strings, and I was confident that he would do good work.

At first, I really wasn't sure if I wanted to put my name on another guitar. The initial step was to see if I could come up with a body shape that I liked; once I got over that hump, it just snowballed. But to get back to your point: I wasn't searching for something different. I just have a natural curiosity that varies from day to day. If I started the album today, I'd probably approach it in a completely different manner.

GW: When you played with Steve Morse and Albert Lee in Anaheim, California, at the beginning of the year, you used a Soldano head on stage. Now you're developing a new amplifier with Peavey. Why?

VAN HALEN: Again, it's just fine tuning. Look, the Ernie Ball/Music Man guitar isn't very different from my original guitar, except that it has a front pickup designed to complement my back pickup. One of my major frustrations is that I've never been able to find a front and back pickup combination that sounded good together. I've never used a front pickup because they've never sounded good with my setup. And if I got the front pickup to sound good, then the back pickup would sound like shit. DiMarzio's Steve Blucher and I worked hard to remedy that situation, and I couldn't be happier with the results. The key is that both pickups are completely different, and if you swapped them it would sound really wicked—simply awful.

GW: But back to the amp.

VAN HALEN: It starts with the guitar, goes through the cord and then into the amp. Hopefully, the amp will reproduce what the guitar is designed to do. That's what I'm interested in. I made some previous attempts to have an amp designed for me, but they fell through. One day Hartley Peavey flew me down to his factory in Meridian, Mississippi, with the intention of getting me to use one of his guitars. I told him I didn't need a guitar, but it would be cool if they could design an amp for me. They agreed.

Next, Peavey flew a real nice, down-home Southern guy named James Brown out to California to work with me for a couple of weeks at a time. He'd tinker away, then ask me what I thought. I'd say, "That's not quite it, how about adding another tube." And so on. It's a pretty serious research and development trip for me, and the amp is starting to sound pretty damn good.

To tell you the truth, I don't care how many amps they make or sell. I just want a line of dependable, great-sounding amps for myself. I don't give a damn about the rest.

GW: So what's so special about the Peavey amp?

VAN HALEN: It's very straight-ahead—it doesn't feature chorusing or anything like that. It's just balls-to-the-wall. It's got five different pre-amp tubes, and each gain stage is set up so you get the ultimate amount of sustain without too much fuzz. For once in my life I don't have to rely on a VARIAC. It's really a hot amp. It hasn't blown up on me yet, so I'm really jazzed. We're working on a cabinet, but I'm still waiting on it. For now, I'm running it through my standard Marshall cabinets.

GW: Why change amps? Your legendary Marshall, which you've used since Van Halen, sounds incredible.

VAN HALEN: I'm not sure whether it's that my tastes have changed or if the amp has changed, but I think that my Marshall is starting to fade—it just doesn't sound like it used to. Even Donn Landee started noticing it. So I guess it was time to start looking elsewhere.

GW: It must have been frightening to rely on that old Marshall, knowing that it could blow at any minute.

VAN HALEN: And believe me, it has!

GW: It's always been rumored that that amp was heavily modified.

VAN HALEN: That's bullshit, man! The guys in the band used to say, "Don't tell anybody what you use." I took their advice, but I never really lied that blatantly. [*chuckles slyly*] Basically, I just let people believe what they wanted to believe. The only thing I've ever done is use a VARIAC to lower the voltage to about 89 volts, so I could turn the amp up without blowing it up. It's been re-tubed, but basically it's just a stock amp.

The bottom line is I really think that every guitar sound comes from the player's fingers. I must've told this story on countless occasions: One time Ted Nugent wanted to play through my magic black box—until he found I didn't have one. When he played through my rig, it still sounded like Ted.

GW: Did you use your Marshall for a reference tone when developing the Peavey?

VAN HALEN: No, my reference was my ear. It depends on what side of the bed you wake up. I mean, I just played through the Peavey earlier today and thought, "Hmmm, this sounded better yesterday."

Occasionally, when I'm recording and can't get the sound I want out of it, I'll just turn the studio monitor down so that all I hear is the unamplified guitar. And I'll lay the parts down that way.

GW: Why isn't there a Van Halen live album?

VAN HALEN: What's the point?

GW: Yours is one of the few groups that could make a legitimately great live record, because the band is so spontaneous.

VAN HALEN: I've never heard a tape that I've been completely satisfied with; something always goes wrong during the course of a show. It usually isn't until the last show of any given tour that we finally eliminate all the bugs. I'm always yelling at the road crew to do something. It's always, "Sorry, we'll nail it next gig." And we never do until the last couple of shows, which are usually perfect. Then the comment is something like, "Don't worry, we'll nail it next tour."

Anyway, there's really no such thing as a truly *live* album. I don't know of any live record that hasn't been doctored in some way, unless you buy a bootleg. Even Cream doctored their stuff. Andy Johns told me that "Crossroads" was not one take. He swears that it was put together. I wasn't there so I can't say for sure, but I've heard the same thing from several reliable sources. On the other hand, who cares? It's still great. Let's put it this way—Clapton played it.

GW: Do you ever put solos together via punch-ins in the studio?

VAN HALEN: Hell, yes! I admit it, I'm not proud. "Jump," for example, was punched in. You can hear that there are two distinct parts to that solo. I can't even remember what I played originally. All I remember is the recorded, pieced-together version that everybody knows.

GW: Let's talk about some of the tunes on the new album. The solo on "Judgment Day" sounds premeditated.

VAN HALEN: Yeah, it wasn't a wing-it thing; it was definitely something I set out to do. It's a double-handed thing that I used to do in my live guitar solo. I just took part of it and inserted it. The actual body of the solo is a kind of surf thing that I came up with.

GW: How many takes do you usually do?

VAN HALEN: No more than three.

GW: Do you keep them all?

VAN HALEN: No, and that scared the hell out of Andy. I'd say, "Man, I can beat that take. Just record over it." Andy would always look at me very suspiciously and say, "Ohhh, Eddie, I don't know..." [*laughs*] But really, I never worry about it, because a solo ain't gonna make or break a tune. A solo should just highlight a song.

GW: "Spanked" is frightening. It really stomps.

VAN HALEN: It's actually kind of a joke tune. I mean, c'mon, it's about getting spanked! Let me tell you where the title of that song comes from: Anyone who has ever spent any time in 5150 complains about the placement of our monitor speakers. They're strange because the room used to be a racquetball court—it wasn't designed to be a recording studio. So Andy Johns walked in for the first time and said, "Hey, mate, your speakers sound kind of spanked." "Spanked!" That killed me. When something is beat to shit, it's "spanked." We quickly adopted it into our vocabulary, and Sammy wrote a song about it. I think that's the funniest song on the album, but nobody seems to get it. It's such an odd combination of heavy music and goofball lyrics. A week ago Mo Ostin, the big cheese from Warner Bros., came up here. He listened to that track with a puzzled look on his face, stroking his chin and saying things like, "Gee guys, that's er...nice."

GW: Both "Spanked" and "Pleasure Dome" sound as though they're influenced by Led Zeppelin.

VAN HALEN: It's funny you should mention those songs together, because Al really helped to shape both tunes. He's a total Zeppelin freak, so it's not surprising. I don't mean to downplay Andy's influence, but I think Alex had more to do with the Zeppelinesque touches. He's a very musical guy—he's not just a drummer. In my book he's the baddest. He was the one that suggested using the E-Bow at the beginning of "Spanked." And "Pleasure Dome" would not be on the album if not for Al. At one point it was just three disjointed riffs. He helped me bridge them together.

GW: You and Alex have always had a tremendous musical affinity. Are there any areas where the two of you don't mesh?

VAN HALEN: I'm always screwing around with time, because I never count. The solo in "Poundcake," for example, goes: four bars, another four bars, then two bars. Al kept insisting that it wasn't finished. He likes to count, and I never do. I'm strictly feel.

GW: "Right Now" has an almost gospel feel to it.

VAN HALEN: I can hear Joe Cocker singing that one. I wrote that music quite a while ago, before Sammy joined the band. If there was any other vocalist I'd like to make a record with, it would be Joe. That song has that classic "Feelin' All Right" groove.

GW: What about "316"?

VAN HALEN: That's something I've had for quite a while as well. I played that to introduce my solo segment on the last tour. I also play it a lot to put my son, Wolfy, to sleep at night. The guys dug it and wanted to put it on the record. I decided to call it "316," because that's Wolf's birthday. I used a Gibson Chet Atkins acoustic solid-body steel string on it. I ran it directly into the board and effected it with an Eventide Harmonizer.

GW: "On Top of the World" features the riff you used in the fade-out to "Jump."

VAN HALEN: Wow, you noticed that! I almost didn't put that on the record, because everything else seemed so new and fresh. Andy forced me to put it in. He kept saying, "I love that song. You have to put it on the record." I used my "Hot for Teacher" Gibson Flying V and my Marshall on that tune, which was cool. But, to be honest, we had five other tunes that I would've preferred to use that didn't make it to the album.

GW: "Pleasure Dome" features that clean-but-dirty sound.

VAN HALEN: That was the Steinberger. But there's the difference between what you call "clean" and what I call "clean." That's almost too clean for me. I consciously went for a different sound on that one, because I was using the Steinberger Trans-Trem and it would have sounded too muddy if I used my usual amount of distortion.

GW: But when you analyze it, your sound is not really that distorted.

VAN HALEN: That's true. In fact, a lot of times I'll have friends around and they'll ask me to dirty up my sound. I prefer a cleaner, more open sound with sustain to a dirty sound that just sounds scratchy and buzzy.

GW: "Pleasure Dome" also features one of your very best solos ever. Was that spontaneous?

VAN HALEN: It's an overdub, but I just winged it.

GW: "In and Out" is very bluesy.

VAN HALEN: I think that my overall approach on this album was much more bluesy and traditional. There's not as much of the wacky tapping stuff. Sometimes I almost feel embarrassed for coming up with that shit!

GUITAR WORLD, MARCH 1992

ON TOP OF THE WORLD

It's alive! GUITAR WORLD goes behind the scenes with Ed, Mike, Sammy and Alex to report on Van Halen's lean, mean concert machine.

By Brad Tolinski

TEN REASON WHY Van Halen is the greatest live rock band in the world:

1. EDWARD IS THE WORLD'S GREATEST GUITARIST.

A definite plus.

2. THEY BUY THEIR CLOTHES AT THE GAP.

And since David Lee Roth's departure, they all wear sensible shoes.

3. THEY LOVE THEIR PARENTS.

Bassist Michael Anthony recalls a visit from his mother and father after one of Van Halen's first major performances: "I really wanted to impress them, so I invited them over to my swanky hotel room. When they walked in, I greeted them by totally demolishing a lamp. I just punched it and sent it flying. They completely freaked out. I just smiled and proudly said, 'Yeah. I can do that!' "

4. THEY NEVER FAKE ORGASM.

"I read a concert review of us once where the guy just couldn't believe we were having such a good time," says Edward Van Halen, shaking his head. "I mean, how do you fake having a good time?"

5. THEY ARE MIDDLE CLASS HEROES.

Satanists have Morbid Angel. Big Brother conspiracy freaks have Queensryche. Snot-nosed dirtbags have Skid Row. And the working class has Bruce. Van Halen is for the rest of us suburban trash.

6. THEY RESPECT THEIR AUDIENCE.

In Eddie's view, there are no "good" or "bad" audiences. "There is only one audience—the people that come and see you. And every night we perform for the best audience in the world."

7. THEY HAVE NO DISCERNIBLE TATTOOS.

8. THEY DISRESPECT TOM JONES.

Hey Eddie, how's the show? "What do you mean? This ain't Vegas, and we aren't Tom Jones. It's still the same four goddamn people, and we're playing our new album and some old stuff. There aren't any blow-up things and we don't ride around on anything. We're just trying to have good time, and hopefully everyone else will have a good time too. If that's a show, then we do a helluva show."

9. ANTHONY'S BAR AND GRILL.

Where do you go when your bandmates take extended solos? Mighty Mike's unique response is Anthony's Bar and Grill—a small tent located on his side of the stage that he magically transforms into a complete wet bar, featuring an unlimited supply of Jack Daniels, several strings of colored lights, and two scantily clad lovelies who shake their booties in time to the soloist on stage. If you're lucky, the bassist will greet you with a genial grin, plenty of good whiskey and a packed house of guest luminaries.

10. THEY ARE MADE OF FLESH AND BLOOD.

By eliminating the usual marketing strategies, gossip and hoopla that surrounds most other albums and tours, Van Halen accentuates the fact that they are human beings—not disposable commodities. They may not be the prettiest, the smartest or the most politically correct, but they are real—and that is what makes for great rock and roll.

GUITAR WORLD: Did you see many concerts when you were growing up?

EDWARD VAN HALEN: The first concert I ever saw was Derek and the Dominos with Eric Clapton, at the Pasadena Civic Center. A friend of mine won two tickets from a local radio station and, knowing what a Clapton fan I was, gave them to me and Al. The show wasn't sold out when I got there, so I paid a little extra money, upgraded my tickets and ended up in the sixth row. It was great, even though I wasn't into Clapton as much as I'd been when he was with Cream. I was still carrying a torch for him, but it was wavering a bit. [*laughs*]

To be honest with you, I was expecting something more powerful. If I would've seen Cream, I probably would've been blown away, because that's the era of Clapton that I really loved. The show was more of a Doobie Brothers kind of thing—there was like this tambourine and bongo player. The power wasn't there. I don't want to knock Clapton. It's just that he had shifted gears and I didn't like it as much. But in spite of all that, Al and I tried to get backstage— we were hoping to see the cat walk by. Unfortunately, Eric had left already, but we did get to meet the tambourine player! Swear to God! Al and I cracked up because the guy actually had a little flight case for his tambourine. I'm not kidding, ask Al. [*A grinning Alex Van Halen walks into the room and nods his affirmation.*]

GW: Can you think of a concert that did live up to your expectations?

VAN HALEN: That s a hard one. Al, can you remember any great shows?

ALEX VAN HALEN: How about Grand Funk?

VAN HALEN: Oh yeah, Grand Funk used to kick ass live! I loved Grand Funk. I can still play all their stuff. Black Sabbath, too. People may think this is weird, but Jethro Tull was pretty happening back then— the *Thick as a Brick* tour was amazing.

ALEX VAN HALEN: Did Ed tell you that he brought his binoculars to the Clapton show? We were sitting in the sixth row, but he had to see everything! [*laughs*]

GW: How did you guys prepare for this tour?

VAN HALEN: We rehearsed for three weeks at the Power Plant in Los Angeles. Basically, we used the time to dig up equipment and brush up on some of the old songs. The new tunes were no problem because we had just finished recording *For Unlawful Carnal Knowledge*.

At one rehearsal, Sammy suggested "Cabo Wabo." We ripped into it, but I completely forgot the chorus. Sammy started laughing and said, "That's what you get for writing complicated shit." I'll fix him, though—the whole next album will be nothing but blues in E. [*laughs*] Which is basically what we do, anyway, except I throw in a few tricks to make it interesting. The problem is, I always forget the tricks! I guess that's why we rehearse.

GW: There were quite a few overdubs on the new record. Did that pose any problems when you attempted to recreate the music for live performance?

MICHAEL ANTHONY: Even before we went into "formal rehearsals," Ed, Al and I got together at 5150 and ran through some of the new material, just to see if the overdubs were going to give us any problems. And we were amazed at how well the new songs translated into our live format. We really didn't have to do any rearranging. Everything sounded great.

GW: What kind of rehearsal space did you rent?

ANTHONY: We used to rent huge rooms, but for the last couple of tours we've kept it more intimate. We just rent a small space, set up our back line, fly the road crew in and run through the set. It's real informal. Right before our first concert we did one rehearsal using our tour stage, just so we could walk up and down ramps. We had to scope out all the slippery spots. [*laughs*] It was more of a safety precaution than anything.

GW: How do you choose which songs to perform?

VAN HALEN: Well, we have four members in the band, plus a manager who thinks he knows what he's talking about [*laughs*], and everybody has an opinion! It's basically a democratic process. Everybody picks their favorites and then we go through a process of elimination. I'm pretty easy. I usually let the other guys pick the songs. We try to change things around and add songs throughout the tour to keep the shows interesting, so eventually we end up playing everybody's favorites.

ANTHONY: All of us were really psyched to play as much of *Carnal Knowledge* as possible. Once we settled on which new songs to play, we just went back and picked a few of the songs that have marked us for life—"You Really Got Me," "Jump," "Finish What Ya Started,"and so on. It was a little harder to choose from our back catalog when Sammy first joined the band, because he didn't feel comfortable with our earlier stuff. If you remember, on our *5150* tour he used to pull someone out of the audience to sing "Jump." But it doesn't really bother him now.

GW: Do you have any general rules when it comes to pacing a concert?

ANTHONY: After we get an idea of the set, we tape every rehearsal so that we can listen to the flow more objectively. Generally, we like to bring the energy way up in the beginning and play two or three songs before Sammy does his first rap of the night. Then it's always a trick to see where to slow things down, or where to insert our solo spots. Then after Ed's solo we like to hit 'em hard until the end of the show. Actually, the pacing usually revolves around Sammy. It has to feel good for him. You can't create a set where your singer is forced to scream at the top of his lungs for a whole evening. He'll burn out by the end of the show or by the end of the tour.

GW: That's something a lot of musicians don't consider—the voice is a very fragile instrument.

ANTHONY: We're probably a little more sensitive to Sammy because we all sing. You have to be considerate, otherwise you can completely trash your singer's throat for a whole tour. Even when we started rehearsing, we'd play a couple of days in a row, then break for a couple of days just so we could slowly get our voices back into shape. Singing in the shower won't really prepare you for a whole tour. [*laughs*]

GW: Do audiences differ?

VAN HALEN: I'd like to explode that myth. There are no "good" or "bad" audiences. There is only one audience—the people that come and see you. And every night we perform for the best audience.

GW: Ed, you described the Meadowlands show in New Jersey as "magic." Why was it magic?

VAN HALEN: I don't know. It's impossible to figure out. That's why I called it "magic."

GW: Are there any differences between playing indoor and outdoor venues?

VAN HALEN: You have a little more freedom to be spontaneous in outdoor venues, because it's easier to get a good sound. If the band decides to break into a new song, we know it won't freak out the soundman.

But you have to be more cautious when playing indoor shows, because the building's acoustics affect everything. It's much harder to get a good sound both onstage and out front in an arena. For example, we just finished our sound check a minute or two ago, and it sounds horrible on stage. That's a problem. If it doesn't sound good to me, I'm not going to throw the sound guy or the band a curve, and I'll tend to be a little less adventurous on stage. But that's not a hard-and-fast rule. At the Meadowlands in New Jersey, Al spontaneously broke into a boogie beat and I started playing "Man With a Mission" in double time, and the whole band picked up on it. And last night we played a bit of "Pleasure Dome," just for the hell of it. We played as much of it as I could remember and then stopped, and went back to whatever it was that we were doing. [*laughs*] You literally have to play it by ear, and see what comes naturally.

On occasion, Sammy will walk over to me in mid-set and say, "Let's not play 'In and Out,' let's play..." whatever, and I won't even question it. He usually has his reasons—sometimes his throat won't be up to it, or he'll just want to blow some phlegm out, or he'll sense something about the audience.

GW: Are you less prone to improvise when you're playing larger venues?

VAN HALEN: The amount of people has nothing to do with it, it has more to do with the sound. If anything, we'd be more prone to improvise in front of a larger audience. Look at it another way—it's more difficult to play to one person. They're either going to like it or not like it. Your chances of having your whole audience hate you is 50-50. But, if you're playing for 80,000 people, at least half are bound to like it. That's 40,000 people behind you. A bigger audience increases the odds of having people on your side. [*laughs*]

GW: More than any other band I can think of, you guys project a great casual bar band vibe even in an arena setting.

VAN HALEN: That's where we started and that's probably where we'll end up. [*laughs*] I mean, I read a review of us once where the guy just couldn't believe we were having such a good time. And I couldn't believe where this guy was coming from. How do you fake having a good time? I'm seriously having a good time up there, and when I'm not, you'll know. I don't think I've answered one of your goddamn questions yet! [*laughs*]

GW: Speaking of bar bands and influences, does the band ever jam on cover songs anymore? You used to do quite a few.

ANTHONY: Oh yeah! It freaks people out. Sometimes during sound check, we'll run through complete catalogs. We'll start by playing Zep's "Dazed and Confused," then break into Cream's "Crossroads." We'll even throw in some Black Sabbath.

GW: Ed, you've been using a Sony wireless system. Is that new?

VAN HALEN: Yeah. As far as I know, I'm the only one on the planet that owns one; it's a prototype. It's the only thing that seems to work for me. The signal-to-noise ratio is excellent. Every other unit I've tried generates too much noise. I play loud and through real amplifiers. It's tough to make something go through the air and not lose anything, or gain any noise. It works great, but it still isn't perfect. We're working on it. For example, when we performed "Spanked" with a six-string bass on the first leg of the tour, the unit couldn't handle it—the delay between hitting a note and hearing the sound was too long, so I used a chord. That was one of the reasons we took the song out of the set. It was a real pain, because we had to make all these special provisions for just one song. Now, I just play one guitar all the way through.

GW: How have your new Ernie Ball guitar and new Peavey amp held up on this tour?

VAN HALEN: Great. I haven't blown an amp yet. The only thing I have done is broken a string here and there. Both are holding up better than anything else I've ever used. I think it's because I've found people that will listen to me and also give me input. I have to thank James Brown from Peavey, Dudley Gimple from Music Man and, of course, Sterling Ball. A lot of my suggestions probably sounded crazy to them, but they had faith in me. They did what I asked and it all worked out well. And now the stuff is road-tested! And let me emphasize that the stuff I'm using is exactly what they're selling in the stores. My rig has not been modified or customized in any way. The Peavey 5150 amp and Ernie Ball/Music Man are not bullshit scams. I'm not putting my name on anything second rate. It's exactly what I use. It's the real shit.

GW: How does the Peavey amp differ from the Marshall on stage?

VAN HALEN: The 5150 is a lot sweeter, has more sustain and is a lot warmer. In a funny way, I don't have to work as hard. I was just searching for something that would reproduce the sound of my fingers and the natural sustain of the guitar and I've found it. I'm not looking for distortion, just a reproduction.

GW: You used to crank your Marshall to 10 across the board. Is it the same with the 5150?

VAN HALEN: No. I have my basic setting, which I'll change slightly, depending on the venue and the stage.

GW: Of the dozen 4 x 12 cabs on stage, how many do you actually use?

VAN HALEN: Three: two wet and one dry. The rest are there as a visual thing, to fill in the holes on stage. I just like the way all those cabinets look.

GW: Is your solo spot still fun for you? It's kind of turned into a "greatest bits."

VAN HALEN: That's intentional. What I really want to do one day is perform each solo in its original context. In other words, do "Eruption" before "You Really Got Me," play the "Little Guitars" solo before "Little Guitars" and so on, as opposed to segregating everything into one big solo section. It just seems like we never have enough time to rehearse something like that, or figure out how to work all those songs into a set. I know that sounds like a bullshit excuse, but we'll do it one day.

GW: Mike, you also have a new rig. Can you tell us something about it?

ANTHONY: Before we started recording the last album, I happened upon someone selling an old '72 Ampeg SVT stack—I always loved the old SVT sound. I compared it to the rig I was using and it sounded so much better it blew me away. Right around that time, Ed was looking for someone to build his new amp. One of the companies he spoke to was St. Louis Music, who manufacture Ampeg amps. Although nothing ever came of Ed's contact with them, I really hit it off with the company. Within a week I had all the bass gear they make shipped over to my house. But it wasn't just their amp heads that impressed me. While I was in St. Louis, I noticed they were making 4 x 10 enclosures with high-frequency horns. I asked them if they ever tried putting horns in their SVT cabinets. They said, "No. But it's a great idea." So they made me a couple of 8 x 10 cabinets with horns, and that's actually what I'm using on stage now. So, essentially, my system consists of an SVT 2 head, a few 300-watt power amps, the custom 8 x 10 cabs with horns, a Rane crossover and four 12-inch port enclosures run at 80 or 90 cycles down for that sub-bass feel. I've got every frequency covered. It's the best sound I've ever had in live performance. I've never been able to feel the punch or the bottom like I do now.

GW: What kind of bass are you using on the road?

ANTHONY: I'm using Music Mans. When Ed started working with them, [*Music Man owner*] Sterling Ball asked me if I wanted to check out one of their basses. I said, "Sure, send one up." Initially I was skeptical, because I had tried some in the early Seventies and found them to be really inconsistent. But I hadn't really checked one out since Sterling took over the company. I was really impressed by the way the bass sounded and played. In fact, we had just started working on the new album and our producer, Andy Johns, said, "Oh man, that sounds amazing." So I used it on a lot of those sessions. Their five-string basses are also good; I used one on "Spanked." A lot of five-strings sound real loose, but the Music Man retained its punch even on the lowest notes.

GW: Are your basses modified in any way?

ANTHONY: I asked Sterling to do two things: shave the neck down a little bit so it would feel more like a Fender Jazz bass, and carve the cutaway a little deeper so it would be easier to access the upper frets. I usually have my necks customized to feel like they're right between a Jazz and a P-bass. I like the feel of a Fender Jazz bass neck, but they're a little too narrow right at the first fret.

GW: Ed, you aren't playing keyboards on this tour. How are the live keyboard sounds produced?

VAN HALEN: During our initial rehearsals I played all the keyboard parts into a sequencer. In fact, you'll notice that the parts sound a little different, and that there are a few mistakes here and there. I wanted the sequenced parts to capture an actual live performance, so there is no touching up or quantizing. No one can say that it ain't me playing.

GW: Is it hard to play to a sequence?

VAN HALEN: I don't really play to the sequence. It's more Al's problem: He hears a mix of the keyboards in his headphones and plays to the synth, and I play to Al. I have a keyboard mix in my monitors, but it's not as crucial as hearing the drums.

GW: What do you hear in your side-fill monitor?

VAN HALEN: Just Al, pretty much. Let's put it this way—I can't play unless I hear Al. The rest sort of matters, but not really. Even if I can't hear my guitar, I'll survive if I can still hear Al.

GW: How do you hear yourself?

VAN HALEN: In front of my onstage cabinets I have a sweet spot that I move in and out of. I also have a little bit of my guitar in the side fills. What really flips me out sometimes is when the lights go out in between songs and I can't see my guitar neck! [*laughter all around*] No, no, no! It's not funny, man. Certain halls are darker than others, and it's harder than hell to see where I'm supposed to be for the next song.

GW: The stages in arena shows tend to be huge. Is it difficult to play as a band when you're as much as 40 feet apart from each other?

ANTHONY: Actually, the stage on this tour is much narrower than that of our previous tour, but I know what you're getting at. We try to keep our mic stands tight so that we maintain that connection. But it's funny: At this point, I can be on the other side of the stage, or on one of the risers, and look at Ed and be right there in the groove and still have that thing flowing.

GW: Ed, I noticed you pulled out your old MXR Phase 90 for "You Really Got Me."

VAN HALEN: I never lost it! I've used it on every tour. I just don't use it as much. It's the same one I used on the first record.

GW: How do you stay sane while on the road?

ANTHONY: ESPN and MTV. [*laughs*] Actually, I have to get out of the hotel room or else I go stir crazy. If we have a day off and we're anywhere remotely near an amusement park, I'll go. I love roller coasters and all that stuff.

GW: Don't you have any problems with being recognized?

ANTHONY: Not really. I just put my hair in a pony tail and put my shades on. I'm kind of lucky because I don't really stand out in a crowd like, say, Sammy. I just grab a couple of guys from the road crew and go. I also think people aren't really expecting to see a member of Van Halen walking around, so they don't really look for you. Every once in a while I'll hear someone say, "Is that…? Nahhhh." If someone does recognize me, they'll usually say something like, "Alex, how are ya?" It's that dreaded rhythm section syndrome. I get called Alex all the time! And frankly, I don't think I'm as ugly as Alex. [*laughs*] Then they'll say, "Hey man, where's Van?" And I'll have to say something like, "He's back at the hotel, resting up for the show."

GW: I was surprised to discover that "Pleasure Dome" was not in the set. It's one of your most powerful songs.

VAN HALEN: I'm surprised too. I guess that's why I started playing it the other night in the middle of the set. [*laughs*] It's a tough song to pull off onstage vocally, because the verses are spoken—that kind of thing doesn't usually translate well in big venues. If people aren't familiar with the tune they'll say, "What the hell is this?" You have to understand. When people come to a concert, they aren't entering places that are designed for music—they're usually designed for sports. We play hockey rinks, for crying out loud.

GW: During the course of a typical Van Halen show, a lot of stuff gets thrown on stage. Does that freak you out?

VAN HALEN: Hell yes, especially those glow-in-the-dark green things. Those hurt like hell. I remember one time in the early days, somebody threw a cherry bomb and it landed in Al's kit and blew a hole through his bass drum. It put him completely out of commission.

GW: Mike, what's your worst road experience? Any brushes with death?

ANTHONY: Once, Craig, my guitar tech, forgot to bring my bottle of Jack Daniels to the gig. [*laughs*] He almost lost his job!

GW: C'mon. Seriously.

ANTHONY: Things are pretty safe these days. The worst of it happened years ago. I can remember we had some problems on the first tour, back in '78. It was the first time Ed and Al had ever been on a plane, and right after take-off the pilot announced that they were having electrical problems or something and the plane was going to have to fly out over the ocean, dump its fuel and then fly back to the airport. Man, everybody was just gripping their seats! Another time we were landing in New York when the pilot realized that there was another plane on the runway. We thought, "This is it." But he managed to pull the plane back up. Other than that, it's been pretty smooth.

GW: Any good road stories?

VAN HALEN: [*Sammy Hagar enters the room*] Sammy can help us out with that one. Sammy and I have gotten so tight on this tour, we're like brothers. Seriously. We were just hanging out the other night getting completely sloppy—hugging and stuff. It's so great having a cat like this to work with.

SAMMY HAGAR: In terms of road stories, I'd have to say it doesn't get any better than just hanging like we did last night. I've felt a lot on this tour. The band is really communicating on a very meaningful level now; I think it's really beginning to translate in the music. That's exciting.

VAN HALEN: When I first met Sammy, I'd go up to him and give him a hug and a kiss because I was happy to see him, and he'd tighten up a little bit. Now he comes up to me and gives me a hug. That's great. Not that this one isn't, but the next record is going to be a real motherfucker.

GW: How does touring these days compare to, say, 10 years ago?

VAN HALEN: In the old days, I had my rig set up in the back section of our tour bus and I'd just play, play, play. Now I have a wife and kid. I'm not saying that I'm not into the music as much, but there are other things in my life. That's why we didn't crank out another record after *OU812*. Even though music is my life, my life is not completely music. Even now, we'll probably take off for at least a year or two before the next record. Maybe I'll have another kid. But it's funny, the older you get, the quicker time passes. I'm not saying I feel old. In my heart I'm still 18, and I think it comes out in the music. I love the volume, I love the power, and I love rock and roll. For example, I sprained my ankle last night, so I probably won't jump as much tonight. But halfway through the show, I'll probably forget all about it.

Ebet Roberts

Les Paul and Edward Van Halen

GUITAR WORLD, NOVEMBER 1995

ED'S WOOD

Eddie Van Halen discusses his new signature line of Peavey guitars.

By Tom Beaujour

"I WAS SO closely involved with the development of these guitars that it's almost like I built them myself," says Edward Van Halen, as he cradles a prototype of his Peavey guitar.

"I'm going to name it after my son, Wolfgang," continues Eddie, who is, in fact, beaming down at the Peavey like a proud father. The new guitar, which will be available to the public as soon as Van Halen has given it his final stamp of approval, is not a radical departure from the Music Man guitars that currently bear the guitarist's name. "Basically, it's just a natural evolution of the Music Man guitar," says Van Halen. "I just blew it out on the top horn and the lower bout a bit and changed the location of the toggle switch, because it seemed to get in my way where it was on the old guitar."

The positioning of the toggle switch on the new guitar may be fairly standard, but any guitar played by Edward is sure to boast a few quirky departures from tradition. "Les Paul players might find this to be odd, but the toggle switch is reversed so that the up position selects the bridge pickup and the down position selects the neck. I did that because when I tap and the toggle is in the down position, I sometimes bump it up with my arm. I figured, 'Whoever made the rule that down has to be the rear pickup? Fuck that shit, for me it's better the other way.' "

While the final details of the new Peavey guitar could very well change before the instrument goes into production, much of the guitar's fundamental design characteristics are in place. Like Edward's Music Man, the Peavey will likely have a basswood body with a maple top. The top, however, will be arched and contoured, a refinement of the Music Man's Telecaster-inspired flat face. Like the Music Man, the guitar will probably have a bird's-eye maple neck and a locking Floyd Rose-licensed system. The Peavey tremolo, however, features a new Van Halen-patented pitch-dropping device on the low E string that will make a grunge-friendly drop-D tuning instantly accessible. "I use it on all the songs with that tuning," says Van Halen. " 'Don't Tell Me What Love Can Do,' 'Amsterdam,' 'Unchained'—it's easy as pie. 'Poink,' you're down and 'poink,' you're back up. It's going to come standard on the guitar."

Peavey and Van Halen plan to release several models of the guitar including a standard model that will list for approximately $1200, a limited edition neck-through body version that will list for about $1800, and an entry level guitar for beginners that will command a paltry $400 dollars. And while the new guitars, which Van Halen plans to use exclusively once they are perfected, are certainly intended for mass consumption, the guitarist stresses that they were developed to suit only one man's taste. "It's hard to design a guitar for everyone, so I designed a guitar for myself," says Edward. "If anyone happens to want one, then here it is."

GUITAR WORLD: Did you talk to any other guitar manufacturers before going with Peavey?

EDWARD VAN HALEN: No. Although Gibson's Henry Juszkiewicz did come to our Nashville show. I thought that he just wanted to say hello, but he actually wanted to discuss a deal. I was like, "Dude, you're about six months too late. [*laughs*] I've been working with Peavey." So he goes, "Well, what's your deal like?" And I said, "Well, it's my guitar, my design, I own it and Peavey builds it for me. I own everything, so if I ever leave Peavey—which I don't anticipate, because Hartley Peavey is just the greatest guy and we get along like friends, just like Sterling Ball and I are—then I take it with me.

GW: Have you ever been tempted to use a classic vintage instrument like an old Les Paul or a Strat?

VAN HALEN: No, there's really no point. The electric guitar has not changed a fucking bit since Leo Fender and Les Paul. I get the same sounds out of my guitars that I get out of a Les Paul or any other humbucking-style guitar, and when I come out with the single-coil version I have planned, I'll be able to get the same sounds out of that that I can from a Strat. For Les Paul fans, there's also going to be a non-tremolo version of the Peavey, probably available with or without the piezo pickup that my prototype is equipped with.

GW: When did you make the decision to move from Music Man to Peavey?

VAN HALEN: When I started realizing what the drawbacks of working with a small company are, such as problems with product availability. Before I left Music Man, I had my management call 15 Music Man dealers from Ohio to Hawaii to find out how long the waiting period was to get one of my guitars. The shortest time quoted was 10 months, but most dealers said it could take anything from a year to a year and a half. Everywhere I went, kids were telling me, "I can't get your guitar!" Some kid is not going to shell out the $1800 that guitar costs and then wait 18 months to get it! That's the reason I left.

I'm not in the business of making guitars—that's not my livelihood. I make music for a living. I didn't go with Music Man for the money, and I didn't change companies for the money either—contrary to popular belief. People think I got a big lump of money from Peavey or something, but that had nothing to do with the switch. I went with Music Man in the first place because of their ability to produce a quality instrument. My experience with my 5150 amps proved Peavey's commitment to have extremely strict quality control as well. So the most logical home for me to go to was Peavey, especially after we got the combo unit finished.

If anything, the new guitars are as good or better quality as the

Music Mans because of the contoured top, which is more difficult and expensive to make. On top of that, the guitar's going to sell for about $500 less than the Music Man.

GW: Is the lower price tag of the new guitar a result of the enormous production resources at Peavey's disposal?

VAN HALEN: Yeah. So if anything, I moved to Peavey to give whoever wants one of my guitars a better opportunity to have one. We're actually going to come out with three models: a neck-through-body version, which will cost about as much as the bolt-on Music Man; the bolt-on version that I have with me today, which will cost around $1200; and a cheap version for kids who are just starting to learn how to play—which will be $300 or $400.

GW: Will the budget version be an import?

VAN HALEN: No. All the guitars will be made in the U.S. That's actually another reason I wanted to go with Peavey. America can mass produce a good guitar. They don't have to be made in Japan or Korea or in a small shop like Music Man. A big company can do it if they do it right, and they're doing it right.

GW: You've long been associated with bolt-on-neck guitars, so it seems unusual for you to endorse a neck-through design.

VAN HALEN: It'll be a special edition, limited run thing. Obviously, I generally haven't played neck-through guitars. I always played piece-of-shit guitars that I made myself, because I used to jump around so much that I would break necks off all the time, and it's easier to just screw another one on than to build a whole new guitar!

GW: As you mentioned, Peavey also makes your 5150 amplifiers. Were the new guitars built to work optimally with those amps?

VAN HALEN: Nope. They're just built to my ear. And to be quite honest, I'm not completely happy with them yet. The guitars I have are just prototypes.

GW: How do they differ from what the final version will be?

VAN HALEN: The bodies on the guitars I have are made out of poplar instead of basswood, which is what the Music Man is made out of.

But to tell you the truth, I'm not sure what the final version will be like. It's not a done deal—yet. I mean, I'm definitely working with Peavey, and that's a done deal, meaning that I'm not going to work with any other company. The guitar will definitely have the body shape it has now, but whether it has a solid body color, or a nice curly, flame-maple top really depends on the sound. When you start adding maple to the equation, it really changes the tone of a guitar, and the countoured—as opposed to flat—maple top also changes the sound. We're still right in the middle of it. Hopefully, by the time the National Association of Music Merchants show rolls around in January, it'll be ready.

GW: Do you think you'll actually be able to have a flamed maple top and keep the price down?

VAN HALEN: If not, then I'll just go with solid basswood and have it contoured, but use solid colors. I don't give a fuck what the guitars look like; I want them to sound good. If it's a solid color, it's a solid color—and if it's a nice curly maple design, that's fine, too. It's gotta sound good.

GW: Your protoype models have two knobs on them, as opposed to the one-knob setup you used on your Music Man and on guitars you had before that.

VAN HALEN: I haven't decided yet whether the final version will have two knobs or not. But if it does, it will be a volume control for each pickup, not a tone and a volume.

GW: Hartley Peavey says he wants you to put a tone control in the guitar because it would make the instrument more versatile.

VAN HALEN: Yeah, but you just don't need a fuckin' tone control! I told Hartley I would split the difference with him on an extra knob, but it would be a volume control. That way you can execute dynamic changes from pickup to pickup by just flipping the toggle switch. So Hartley and I did have a little head butt about that, but ultimately it's my guitar, and that's the deal.

GW: I'm sure there will be speculation that working with a big company like Peavey means you'll have to make more concessions, like adding an extra knob, to promote the mass marketability of the guitar.

VAN HALEN: Not at all. I have complete control over the guitar, and that's why they're not out yet. Peavey wanted to show the guitars at the Nasville NAMM show in July, and I told them, "No way. It ain't going to come out until I say it's ready. And that's just the way it is. I don't put my name on anything unless I'm completely happy with it—just like the combo amp. In fact, what's funny is that you guys reviewed the combo amp [Guitar World, *June 1995*] before it had final approval. The clean channel is ten times better now then it was then. At first I was like, "Yeah, yeah it's good." And then I was like, "No, I can't use it." So we tweaked it again. Now on stage I'm using the 5150 heads for my dirty sounds and the combo amps for my clean sound.

GW: The new guitar has an interesting drop-D device for the low-E string.

VAN HALEN: That's my latest gadget. I own the patent for it along with the guy who designed it, Adam Reiver. It wraps around the bolt that you use to lock in the string, and you just pop it out to drop the string's pitch. The unit is fine-tunable so as to accommodate any variation in the bolts, which sometimes aren't machined exactly to spec. If you wanted to, you could have six of these and be able to drop your whole guitar to a different tuning.

GW: Will this device be available on other Peavey guitars as well?

VAN HALEN: I'm not sure about that. I own it, so it depends if Hartley wants to pay me or not! [*laughs*] But it will be available as an accessory for other people whose guitars have Floyd Rose bridges.

GW: You worked very closely with DiMarzio's Steve Blucher on the pickup design for the Music Man Guitars. Are those pickups going to be in this instrument as well?

VAN HALEN: I don't want to bad mouth anybody or get into any stink here, but somehow behind my back, Music Man ended up owning those pickups instead of me—which is bullshit, because it was my ear, not Music Man, that made Blucher design those pickups the way they are. Since I can't use those, Jim D'acola and I started from scratch again, and the new pickups are great. To tell you the truth, I'm glad that I couldn't take the old pickups, because I like the sound of the new ones better.

GW: What are the characteristics that you look for in a pickup?

VAN HALEN: A warmth, sustain and not too much annoying 10k high end. Something fat-sounding, but not too muddy on the low end.

GW: In other words, something that sounds good.

VAN HALEN: Yeah! [*laughs*] But everyone's opinion of what's "good" is different, so I'm going by my ear.

GW: Are the pickups on the new guitar mounted directly into the body like they are on the Music Man?

VAN HALEN: Yes. I truly believe—and always have—that everything has to be connected. I don't like floating tailpieces, and I don't like the pickups floating. Everything has to be drilled into the wood, because that's where the sustain comes from.

GW: Will the dimensions of the neck on the Peavey guitar be copied from those of the neck of your 5150 Kramer, like the neck on the Music Man was?

VAN HALEN: You can't patent something like that, so yes, I'm going to make it comfortable for my hand and make it easy to play.

GW: Has having the new guitar inspired you to write any new songs?

VAN HALEN: Big time. We were just on tour in Europe and Peavey sent me a guitar out there. I ended up writing four new tunes on it.

GW: What kind of material have you been coming up with?

VAN HALEN: I don't know! That's like asking me what the difference between the first album and *Balance* is. I can't tell you that because I just write what comes to me.

GW: The last time we spoke [Guitar World, *Feb. 1995*], you had recently quit drinking. Have you been succesful in staying dry?

VAN HALEN: Oh yeah. It's been 10 months and then some. I feel great.

GW: Do you think your playing on this tour has benefited from your sobriety?

VAN HALEN: I think my playing is way better. I'm just so much more aware. I feel alive. It's like being on my first tour ever.

GW: Are you getting the jitters a lot more now?

VAN HALEN: Oh yeah. I get nervous every night. That's why I used to drink.

GW: The nervousness must be very difficult to overcome without a crutch.

VAN HALEN: I have to overcome it every night. I'll be out there tonight and I'll be nervous. But halfway into the set I'll loosen up and be like, "What the fuck?"

Being nervous is the strangest thing, because sometimes I'm not and sometimes I am. We did Letterman the other night, and I have never been so nervous in my life! And I'm thinking to myself, "Why? What's the point of being nervous?" But then again, I guess I wouldn't be human if I wasn't.

GUITAR WORLD, FEBRUARY 1995

CUT AND DRY

Edward Van Halen trims his hair, quits drinking and regains his BALANCE.

By Tom Beaujour with Greg Di Bennedetto

EDWARD VAN HALEN welcomes me to 5150, his legendary 24-track home studio, with a handshake and a slap on the back. But for a split second I am unable to return the warm greeting, as I am dumbstruck: Standing in front of me, it seems, is not Edward, but his evil twin.

The guitarist's moppish hair has been lopped off, leaving in its place an expertly styled flattop. Van Halen's soft-featured face, once frozen into a perpetually boyish grin, has been hardened by a newly-sprouted goatee. When I gather the courage to ask what prompted this drastic makeover, Edward's response is amiable.

"I lost a golf bet with [*Buffalo Bills quarterback*] Jim Kelly, and ended up having to shave my head with a fucking Norelco Razor," he explains. "I just decided to leave it short, because I was sick of having long hair."

The fact is, Edward is a changed man in far more significant ways than his choice of 'do. For the most part, the guitarist has abandoned the pyrotechnic guitar antics that rocketed him to prominence 17 years ago, opting instead for a more lyrical, restrained approach to his instrument. More significantly, Edward, who will turn 40 in January, is the father of a three-and-a-half-year-old son,

Wolfgang, and he takes his role as a parent extremely seriously. Unlike many celebrities whose involvement with their children extends only to child-support payments, Edward lovingly subjects himself to the unglamorous but rewarding rigors of everyday parenting. "Wolfie wakes us up at six in the morning, saying, 'Come on, you're mine, Daddy. I want to do this. I want to do that,' " he says with a doting smile. "I take him to school every morning."

No sooner have I dispensed with the pre-interview pleasantries when Edward whisks me into the studio's control room. As he prepares to crank up the band's soon-to-be-released album, *Balance* (Warner Bros.) on the studio's ear-annihilating monitors, Van Halen pauses, his finger poised on the CD player's "play" button.

"You know," he says with a concerned look, "you should probably listen to this in the car because it sounds much better in there. We mastered this record differently than the last one, and it sounds more ballsy—except in here."

Tempted as I am by the offer to hang out in one of Edward's many fine automobiles, I politely decline, opting to remain in the more spacious and well-lit environment of the control room. "Well, okay," says Eddie. "Here we go!"

The album opens with an ominous Tibetan monk chant sample which gives way to the lush, heavy layers of "Seventh Seal." Suddenly the music stops. "You have to listen to this in the car," says Edward. "It really sounds better."

Moments later, the two of us are seated in what must be the Van Halens' new family car, a charcoal-gray Mercedes sedan. In spite of the vehicle's austere looks, the stereo system is brutally loud, and *Balance*'s wave of guitar goodness swallows us alive. Edward sits quietly, his eyes closed as he basks in the glory of his own creation. Periodically, he wakes from his deep-listening trance to point out a particularly noteworthy lick or explain the origin of a song. Apparently, Van Halen's success has not lessened the mixture of excitement and apprehension that he, like most musicians, feels when unveiling a just-completed piece of work.

Consistent with Edward's new-found maturity are his most

recent efforts to put an end to his well-documented drinking habit. "I think that God gave me one big bottle of alcohol and I drank it real fast," he says. "God gives everyone a bottle when they're born, and they have to make it last a lifetime. Well, I drank mine too quickly, so I just can't drink anymore."

Surprisingly, Edward, who will consume several non-alcoholic beers during the course of the interview, is more than willing to discuss the topic of his drinking at great length.

Although it may come as a shock to some, hard rock's perennial whiz kid has become a man.

GUITAR WORLD: Was all of the new album recorded here at 5150?

EDWARD VAN HALEN: Almost everything was done here, except for five lead vocal tracks, which were recorded in Vancouver.

GW: Why did you go there?

VAN HALEN: Because Bruce Fairbairn, our producer, lives up there. He would fly down every Monday morning and we'd work during the week. On the weekends, he'd go home. We had promised him before we began recording that we'd do some vocals up there so that he could be with his family a little more.

GW: It seems awfully adult for Van Halen to be sticking to the kind of rigid recording schedule you're describing.

VAN HALEN: Bruce is very structured. He wouldn't let us loaf for a minute, so we completed *Balance* more quickly than any other album we've done in years. We wrote, recorded and mastered the whole fucking thing in five months. We started in June, and by the end of October it was mastered.

GW: What kind of pre-production work did you do to prepare for the recording of *Balance*?

VAN HALEN: We demoed about 20 songs for Bruce. Actually, we over-cut! There are like four songs that aren't even on the record. It just got too long. We had an hour's worth of music in the can, and Bruce said, "Do you want to do a double CD or what?"

GW: How did you decide which songs should go on the record?

VAN HALEN: Well, out of, say, 20 songs, the ones that got finished first ended up on the record.

Sometimes, when I focus on writing, I start blazing: I'll come up with all kinds of shit and it overwhelms Sammy for a bit. The way he works best is when he focuses on one thing and writes lyrics for it. So, since I was writing so much, a lot of lyrics weren't done. For example, for the instrumental track, "Baluchitherium," we were actually working on lyrics and we ended up going, "Fuck it, it sounds pretty good without vocals," so we left it. And Sammy was relieved— "Okay, I got one less to work on." So, yeah, there are actually four more tunes that the music is finished for. We'll finish those for the next record, or whenever.

GW: Even though you made the album so quickly, the song arrangements seem more thoughtfully developed than anything you've done in the past.

VAN HALEN: Yeah, they are. Bruce just said, "Work, motherfuckers." He's a serious guy. He walks in with his briefcase and says, "This is what we're doing today." We would be like, "Oh fuck, I don't want to do it. Let's do that tomorrow." He always answered, "No, you're doing it now." [*laughs*] It was great working with him. We're doing the next record with him, too.

He's a very musical guy. He dabbles in a little bit of everything, plays a little guitar and a little piano, but his main instrument is trumpet. He's producing Chicago right now—a big band horn thing. Bruce isn't like certain producers who spend all their time on the phone and every once in a while ask, "Got it yet?" He's a hands-on guy.

GW: Were you at all worried that Bruce, who produced Aerosmith's last couple of albums, might make the band sound too slick?

VAN HALEN: No. A good producer brings out the best in the artist he's working with. You shouldn't be able to listen to something and say, "So-and-so produced this album." Bruce's stamp is not on our record because a good producer should not have a stamp. People who are only capable of molding a band to fit their "trademark" sound are bullshit producers. Bruce, on the other hand, just enhanced the best parts of what the band already had to offer.

GW: Van Halen recording sessions have in the past been fueled by large quantities of alcohol, but drunkenness and dissipation don't seem to be compatible with Bruce's disciplinarian production style. I notice that right now, at least, you're drinking a non-alcoholic beer. Are you not drinking at all anymore?

VAN HALEN: No, I'm not.

GW: How long has it been since you stopped?

VAN HALEN: It's been off and on. This time about a month. Actually, I did really well while we made the record. I played a lot of stuff sober, which really weirded me out. It took me a while to get into it without the help of the alcohol.

GW: What is it about drinking that facilitates your playing?

VAN HALEN: There's like this wall, and when I drink, my inhibitions are lower so I just wing stuff without getting embarrassed or nervous. But I have to get past that because drinking's no good. I've been doing it too long.

GW: Do you have any insight into why you've had so much trouble stopping?

VAN HALEN: Because I can't stop! I'm an alcoholic. It's like, "Just a couple? Fuck you! I'll drink until I go to sleep."

GW: Your father had a drinking problem as well, didn't he?

VAN HALEN: Yes, but I think my problem is more a product of my environment than any genetic factor. I remember my dad got me drinking and smoking when I was 12. I was nervous, so he said to me, "Here. Have a shot of vodka." Boom—I wasn't nervous anymore. My mom used to buy me cigarettes and it just stuck, it was habit. I don't drink for the taste of it, I drink to get a fucking buzz. I like to get drunk. I really do.

GW: Do you think that the fact that your work schedule is less rigid than most people's has resulted in your drinking more?

VAN HALEN: You know, believe it or not, I drink more when I'm playing and writing and working than when I'm not. I come up to the studio and drink and work. When I go into the house, I don't drink. If I spend a weekend at the beach, I don't drink. So it's really funny.

GW: It's definitely uncommon.

VAN HALEN: For me, leisure time is not the problem area. My problem is that I go to the office to drink. It's completely ass-backwards. And the only reason I keep doing it is because it still works, believe it or not. It just breaks down the inhibitions. And I'm too inhibited, ordinarily—I get real nervous.

GW: You said you recorded most of *Balance* sober.

VAN HALEN: Yeah, but sometimes, I would listen back to something and go, "Ooh, that's stiff. Let me redo that."

GW: Uh-oh.

VAN HALEN: But I didn't drink too much. When we made the last record, I had at least 12 to 15 beers in me each day. This time, nobody but me drank while we were working. And if I got a little bit overboard, I'd say "I'm out of here, I'm too far gone," and call it a day.

Do you know what I've noticed that's funny? When I'm really tired, I feel the same as when I'm drunk, because it's easier for me to get through to the other side, or whatever you want to call it. It's easier for me to just let go and not judge what I'm doing. It's all about just opening up and being free. But if I'm drinking I don't even think about it. It's like, "Oh, I made a mistake, big fucking deal."

GW: Overall, *Balance* seems to be a darker record than *For Unlawful Carnal Knowledge* and its immediate predecessors. What inspired you to write the music?

VAN HALEN: I don't really know what inspires me to write the music I do, but usually, the music will set the tone for the lyrics. I don't think it's really that dark. The first tune, "Seventh Seal," is kind of that way, but "Can't Stop Loving You" is an awesome rock groove.

GW: There are more songs written in minor keys than on the last record.

VAN HALEN: D minor. Everything's in D minor, the saddest of all keys.

GW: While we were listening to the record a little while ago, you indicated that you recorded the strange piano piece, "Strung Out," back in the early Eighties.

VAN HALEN: Yeah, I forget exactly what year that was, but it was before '84. Valerie [*Bertinelli, Edward's wife*] and I had rented [*popular composer, pianist and arranger*] Marvin Hamlisch's beach house for the summer. I just used to waste this beautiful piano. It was like a Baldwin or a Yamaha. It had cigarette burns all over it and I was sticking everything but the kitchen sink in it: ping-pong balls, D batteries, knives, forks—I even broke a few strings.

I don't know what prompted me to do it. I was just fucking around. Actually, it started off with me playing the strings with my fingers. I would create harmonics by hitting the key and muffling the string up and down to bring harmonics out like on a guitar. I have like 10 tapes of this stuff, and Bruce picked out this little part. He loved it.

GW: Was Hamlisch furious when he returned to his house?

VAN HALEN: Yeah, he was. I tried to get the piano fixed before he came back, but he found out somehow. I guess they didn't repaint it as well as they could have.

GW: You feature an acoustic guitar very prominently on "Take Me Back," one of the tracks off the new album. What finally prompted you to go "unplugged," if only for a moment?

VAN HALEN: I actually wrote that ditty a while ago. I wanted to put it on the last record, but we never really completed it. This time around I really wanted to finish the song, because I still really liked it. So we worked it up.

GW: What kind of acoustic did you use?

VAN HALEN: It's a South American guitar called a Musser. I bought it at [*L.A. vintage shop*] Norm's Rare Guitars.

GW: Other than using an acoustic, did you do anything else out of the ordinary for the album?

VAN HALEN: Nope. As usual, I have two Shure SM-57s miking one cabinet. Pretty much everything was recorded with the 5150 amp, but I did use the old Marshall Super Lead head on about three tunes. The stuff that's real clean-sounding, like "Aftershock," was done with the Marshall.

GW: Why did you decide to use the Marshall again?

VAN HALEN: Just to get a different sound.

GW: A few years ago, you were convinced that the amp had faded beyond the point of usefulness.

VAN HALEN: I think I just got tired of it. Just recently, this Dutch guy named Peter cleaned the amp for me and restored it to its totally original state. Even though I never had the amp modified, a bunch of parts had been replaced over the years.

I've also got a Peavey 5150 combo unit coming out in January. It's 60 watts and has two 12-inch speakers and a sealed back. It's a bad-ass little amp. It just shits all over every other combo on the market—at least in my opinion. I've been working on the amp for the last year because I wanted it to have a really good clean channel, because most people who want a combo amp need it to be versatile.

Of course, I wanted the main sound to be happening, as well. That also took a lot of work, because the amp's electronics had to be packed into a smaller box, with the controls on top. When you start changing wire lengths around like we had to, it usually affects the sound, so it took Peavey's tech, James Brown, a while to perfect it.

GW: Even though this record has a drier sound than *For Unlawful Carnal Knowledge*, the guitars still have that chorus-y shimmer that's become a staple of your sound lately. Do you double most of your rhythm tracks?

VAN HALEN: No, not at all. But everything has the Eventide harmonizer on it. The dry guitar signal is on the left, and the duplicate sound that the Eventide generates is on the right. I barely use the harmonizer as an effect; it's just to split my guitar to both sides of the stereo spectrum. I have it set to detune to 98, so it harmonizes just a little.

GW: When did you start splitting your signal like this?

VAN HALEN: I think *Fair Warning*, or the album after. Maybe *5150*. I forget. But that's been my thing ever since.

In the old days, Donn Landee [*engineer on every Van Halen album from* Van Halen *(Warner Bros., 1978) through* OU812 *(Warner Bros., 1988)*] would have my dry signal on the left and a little echo or reverb on the right. And I'm going, "Well, why don't we use the harmonizer and get the whole fucking guitar over there instead of just [*makes breathy noise to imitate the decay of a reverb or Echoplex unit*] the tail end of everything I play. I hated that sound.

GW: Really? I always thought of it as a really cool trademark of your sound.

VAN HALEN: I can't stand it. I guess it worked for the first record. But after that it got old really fast. If you have a car and the left speaker's blown, the guitar is gone. If you're sitting on the right in the back seat, you don't hear the guitar even if both front speakers work. What kind of shit is that?

GW: It sounds like you have your guitar plugged into a Leslie on "Not Enough."

VAN HALEN: We plugged the Marshall into the Leslie via this preamp box that my tech, Matt Bruck, brought over. He had used it on the demo tape for his band, Zen Boy. He hooked me up and I just played it.

GW: What inspired the solo on that song?

VAN HALEN: I was hearing a Beatles-ish feel, so I went for a "While My Guitar Gently Weeps" kind of thing.

GW: The songs on *Balance* seem to have more key changes than your previous work.

VAN HALEN: It's called "better songwriting." [*laughs*]

GW: Has your piano training given you an increased understanding of harmony, which in turn helps your songwriting?

VAN HALEN: Yeah, totally.

GW: You play some barrelhouse piano on "Big Fat Money," but besides that, there aren't very many keyboards on *Balance.* Is there a reason for that?

VAN HALEN: Yeah, I haven't really spent that much time playing piano lately. I think that old synth sound didn't feel right for this record. I might use it in the future, though. Who knows.

GW: "Big Fat Money" has an unusual solo that's almost humorous. What prompted that radical departure from your usual style?

VAN HALEN: That was Bruce's idea. He's going, "Hey, let's go for a jazz sound." And I'm going, "Okay." So I pulled out an old 335, ran it through my Marshall set really low and just did it. It's funny.

GW: At the end of the instrumental track "Baluchitherium," there's an entire menagerie of guitar sounds.

VAN HALEN: That's exactly what it is. It sounds like a bunch of animals—like a zoo. There's a bunch of birds and chirps and dinosaur calls and the elephant sounds I've always made. It just felt like a fun thing to do. You can even hear my dog Sherman howling on there.

GW: What mic did you use on the dog?

VAN HALEN: Uhhh, a Sennheiser. [*laughs*] We have pictures of it too; it's so funny. We had to tape a hot dog to the microphone. Swear to God. The dog was afraid of the mic. We kept pushing him up there and he'd back off. So we taped the hot dog to it, and then started making a bunch of noise. We actually bought a tape of a fire engine. We'd play the tape, and Sherman would get up to the mic, sniff the hot dog and bark.

GW: In addition to the dog and the other animals, it also sounded like there was some six-string bass on that song.

VAN HALEN: Actually, no. You know what I used? It was a Music Man Albert Lee model guitar that I strung with heavier strings and tuned down to low A.

GW: What does "Baluchitherium" mean?

VAN HALEN: Actually, Valerie tipped me to it. When she heard the song for the first time, she said, "That sounds like a dinosaur song," because it sounds so big. She started looking through a book and said, "How about 'baluchitherium?' " And I'm going, "What the fuck is that?" I started reading, and it turns out that the baluchitherium was the biggest mammal that lived in the prehistoric age. Valerie always titles songs. She titled "1984."

GW: It's surprising you don't really solo over the track, since there are no vocals in the way.

VAN HALEN: I just wanted a simple melodic feel. Even if there were to be a solo, it would only diverge from the melody a little bit. A lot of times, if there's a melody there, I prefer to stick to it, or maybe play with it a little, as opposed to indulging in gymnastics.

It comes back to the same old question people are always asking me: "When are you going to do a solo record?" Well, if I did, it would probably be similar to "Baluchitherium," meaning it would be Van Halen music—which I write anyway—but without singing.

I wouldn't do all the loony gymnastic shit. What's the point? That stuff goes in one ear and out the other.

GW: It appeals to a select group of people.

VAN HALEN: Yeah, I mean, who can play the fastest, who can do this, who can do that. Fuck, who cares? I stopped doing that years ago. On this album, I focused on fitting the song. For example, on "Take Me Back" I did a little slide ditty that just fit the song, instead of playing an actual solo. "Seventh Seal" has no solo at all. Instead, I added a musical interlude that worked for the song.

On *Van Halen*, I was a young punk, and everything revolved around the fastest kid in town—the gunslinger attitude. But I'd say that at the time of *Fair Warning*, I started concentrating more on songwriting. But I guess in most people's minds I'm just a gunslinger. The thing is, I do so much more than just blow fucking solos. Actually, that's the least of what I do.

GW: To what extent do you think the success of Van Halen still rests upon your skills as a guitar player?

VAN HALEN: I have no idea. I don't analyze it. I try to concentrate on writing good songs and, hopefully, people will like them.

GW: Have you ever considered leaving your unaccompanied solo out of your live shows?

VAN HALEN: I've thought about it many times. Actually, back when Sammy joined the band, I said, "I'm tired of doing fucking guitar solos," but everyone insisted that I had to keep doing them.

GW: Isn't it still a thrill for you to have people focusing on you alone and to hear them scream your name?

VAN HALEN: Yeah, but it's such masturbation. A lot of it is just screaming, "Look at me!" Some parts of the solo, like "Cathedral" or "Eruption," are little compositions, and I don't mind doing those. But, still, what's the point? I get bored doing it.

GW: In one of your previous *Guitar World* interviews, you said that sometimes you're a little embarrassed that you popularized the two-handed tapping technique, because it became such an overused gimmick.

VAN HALEN: I did feel that way, but I don't anymore, because

Jay Blakesberg

nobody's tapping these days.

GW: Even you don't tap as much as you once did.

VAN HALEN: I do it as much as I always have. It's part of my playing. I used it all over the record; you just can't tell. I probably tap a little bit in every song. To me it's a part of my playing, it's not, "Oh, I'm going to do my trick now."

GW: You recently lost your manager and dear friend, Ed Leffler, to cancer. How has his passing affected the band?

VAN HALEN: I hadn't really thought about it. We've got a new manager, Ray Daniels, who also manages Rush, King's X and Extreme. We all miss Ed, but life goes on. I guess it brought us closer. Ed was never involved with any of the music, so when we're in the studio, actually making music, we don't think about him that much. It's just, you know, around his birthday and holidays and everything— that's when you think about him.

GW: Did you take more control of your business affairs in the period of transition between managers?

VAN HALEN: We had to—and, boy, it's a ridiculous job. I would never want to be a manager. You get at least 50 phone calls a day about totally stupid, ridiculous shit.

GW: Were you criticized for "selling out" when you let Pepsi use "Right Now" for their ill-fated Crystal Pepsi advertising campaign?

VAN HALEN: Probably, but the only reason we gave them the music was because they were going to use the song anyway. They would just have recut the song with studio musicians, like they do for some TV movies when they redo an old hit because they can't use the original. If they use the original, they've got to pay, but if they don't, all they do is give credit to the artist and then pay the studio cats. Pepsi told us that they were going to do that, so we said, "Hey wait a minute, we might as well get the money." I ain't that proud, you know. I'm not going to say—"No, go ahead, rip us off. And keep the money too!"

GW: What's a day in the life of Edward Van Halen like?

VAN HALEN: I spend time with my son, Wolfie, and play a bit of golf. Actually, I started to take some lessons last week, because I'm still a hack at it. I don't get out there enough. It's a cool game for life, because when I'm fucking 90, I could still be doing it, so I might as well learn how to play now.

Our whole road crew plays, so on the road, you get to hang with the guys— which is an awful lot of fun. Golf isn't really about hitting the ball, it's more about male bonding. Letting it hang.

GW: Does your son, who you seem to spend much of your time with, play an instrument yet?

VAN HALEN: He likes to beat on Al's drums and he loves piano. The other day, actually, Valerie and I were up above the garage where I keep all of my guitars, looking for something, and Wolfie saw all the guitars and said—he was so decisive—"You know, when I get bigger, I'm going to play the guitar." [*laughs*] It's like, "Okay, take your pick." He said it with such conviction!

Actually, he isn't exposed to that much music because I really don't play in the house. You figure that he'd be doused with music from the minute he wakes up until he goes to bed at night, but no. He has a normal kid life: He watches Barney and Mickey Mouse and all that shit.

GW: So you try and make sure that Wolfie leads a normal life?

VAN HALEN: No, it's just that I'm normal. I don't do anything that out of the ordinary. He hates loud noise so he'll come in here and go, "Daddy, too loud. Too loud!" Yeah, he makes me turn the shit way down. It's really funny.

GW: He knows that you play music, but do you think he understands your "unique" situation?

VAN HALEN: I don't think so. I don't think he's got that yet. Sometimes, I'll say, "I'm going to work now, Wolfie," and he answers, "You mean you go to the studio?" Then he comes here to visit me when I'm trying to write, and I'll be sitting here with my thumb up my ass, smoking cigarettes and plinking around on the guitar. To him, that's what Daddy does for work. He'll put it together later, I guess, but right now he probably sees other people going to work whereas I just take the golf cart up here.

GW: He probably tells his friends at school, "My dad drives a golf cart." Has he ever seen you play live?

VAN HALEN: Oh yeah! He loves it. He's walked out on stage before, not knowing that he really shouldn't. We'll be standing there jamming, and he just walks out. I was doing my guitar solo once, and I was playing "316," which I wrote for him. He came running out while I was playing, and the crowd just went nuts. I thought to myself, "Whoa, fuck man, I must be really putting some muscle into this or something, because normally they don't cheer that loud for this section!" It turned out they were cheering for him. He had the spotlight on him and he was grooving!

GW: Are there aspects of your celebrity that you dislike?

VAN HALEN: Everyone feels like they own a piece of you, and it's like, "Fuck you! You bought the record, right? That's what you own; you don't own a piece of me!"

GW: Do you get recognized as soon as you leave the house?

VAN HALEN: Well, not since I cut my hair. Nobody recognizes me. It's great. Unfortunately, as soon as the album comes out, everyone will know what I look like again.

It comes with the territory. I'm not pissing and moaning about it at all, it's just that you're asking me. It bothers me a little when I'm having dinner with my wife and someone comes over to our table and says, "I really don't mean to interrupt you or bother you..." Just give me the piece of paper so I can sign it, and get the fuck out of here!

One particular episode comes to mind. I was on a plane, headed to do Jim Kelly's "Kelly for Kids" benefit, and this lady asked me for my autograph. I asked who it was for, and she answered, "Say 'To Cindy.'" So I wrote "To Cindy" and my name. She looks at me and says, "Well, I could have done that!" I go, "Well, what the fuck do you want?" Did she want me to write her a book?

GW: Some people seem to have more problems coping with fame than others. Do you think that the constant public scrutiny was one of the causes of Kurt Cobain's suicide?

VAN HALEN: If it was, then why was he in this business? Why didn't he just give all his money to charity and live normally? I think it's so funny how bands say, "We don't want fame and fortune." Well, what do they do this for then?

If you want to be a true artist, then make your music and don't even release it. Put it this way: If fame had Cobain crazed to the point where he offed himself, then he went too far. He should have stopped.

I think the guy was just on drugs, man. I think it was drugs. I don't think he was thinking straight. He was fucked up. It was terrible, man. That's the worst karma a person could have—to off himself. I mean, did he want to come back as an ant, or a fucking turd or something? It actually pissed me off when he did that. He wrote great tunes, and if nothing else, he deprived a lot of people of what he could be doing in the future.

GW: Since we're on the topic of drug use, you mentioned that you weren't absolutely thrilled about Sammy's choice of topic for the song "Amsterdam."

VAN HALEN: Well, the song is about smoking dope, and I thought the music might have warranted something more...metaphoric. I envisioned something else, but since I don't write lyrics, I'm not one to piss and moan about it.

GW: Did you ask Sammy to try and come up with something different?

VAN HALEN: Yeah, but he liked it, so that was that. You know, he doesn't like everything I do, either. We're not going to fight about it to the point where the song doesn't get put out. It's part of being in a band. You work together, and you can't please everybody all the time.

GW: Now that you're a father and a role model for your son, does it bother you to have songs about drugs on your records?

VAN HALEN: No, not at all. I don't support any kind of censorship. There's just a time and a place for everything.

GW: Have you been approached to do an *MTV Unplugged*?

VAN HALEN: Yeah, but I'm not an unplugged kind of guy. I don't want to sit there and try to play our music on an acoustic guitar. What's the point? I didn't write it on acoustic—I wrote it on electric guitar, and that's the way it's meant to be delivered. If I wanted it to be acoustic, I would have done it that way originally. I'm not going to butcher my music just so I can be the flavor of the month.

GW: What's the best thing about being Edward Van Halen?

VAN HALEN: It's a great feeling for people to like what you do. I do what I like and other people like it. It's a great payoff. How many people get to experience that?

The other day, I was playing golf on a public course in Pasadena with these two old timers, and one guy says, "Shit, man, a bad day on the course is better than any good day at work." And I started thinking, "Well, I guess for you, but I like my work." I'm really lucky, because I really enjoy making music. I don't consider it to be like clocking in and doing a job.

I'm not making light of making music either. It's hard work, but I enjoy what I do—creating something as opposed to making a part for a fucking Impala or something. I'm just lucky to have found that. And that's half of it: me enjoying what I do. The other half is when other people dig it. That's like, "Whoo! Home run!"

GUITAR WORLD, APRIL 1996

BEST OF BOTH WORLDS

Billy Corgan, alternative rock's crown prince,
interviews hard rock's reigning king, Eddie Van Halen.
By Billy Corgan

MAKE NO MISTAKE. Eddie Van Halen can still kick your ass. The man who single-handedly changed the face of rock is still mean, lean and sharp as a tack. And if you dispute the ownership of the crown, try to imagine a world without him. I came to pay my tribute, sneak a peak at that famous Marshall and meet the man I most wanted to be at 17.

BILLY CORGAN: I was very familiar with all the David Lee Roth-era albums through *1984*, but when I prepared for this interview, I listened to everything so my questions wouldn't be just about the past. What struck me about the Sammy Hagar-era albums was that there was a slow but distinct movement away from the kinetic approach of the early albums to a more song-oriented focus. But I sensed that on *For Unlawful Carnal Knowledge* [*1991*] your playing was in a weird place, that maybe you were getting in a rut.

But when I listened to your most recent album, *Balance* [*1995*], it struck me that you sounded like you were really enjoying yourself again. There was more focus and you sounded really energized.
EDWARD VAN HALEN: *For Unlawful Carnal Knowledge* took a year to record; that's why the playing on it might sound somewhat labored.

Balance, on the other hand, was written and recorded in only four months, so the whole process was quicker and more immediate. I also think our producer, Bruce Fairbairn, had something to do with the sense of excitement on *Balance*. Instead of arguing with me, he encouraged me to pursue my own ideas. He was somebody I could relate to. Together we were able to create a vibe.

And creating the right vibe for things to happen is probably the best thing a producer can do. We interviewed so many producers before we started *Balance*, and he was the only one who said, "Hey, waddaya got? Let's listen to some of your new music." The others seemed more interested in trying to impress us with their credits, rather than finding out what we wanted to accomplish. So I'd have to say that, musically, nothing really changed between the two albums, but Fairbairn created an environment where something good could happen.

CORGAN: So after 20 years of recording, what makes you still want to rock?

VAN HALEN: It's because I'm still 16 inside. I still have that passion, and any true musician doesn't do it for any other reason than passion. My motivation has never been financial. Music is what I do. It's the only thing I know how to do.

CORGAN: But don't you ever have to fight yourself to keep your music exciting?

VAN HALEN: Sure. I have my low points. For example, we recently finished a pretty grueling 11-month tour and I was beat to hell. I was depressed. I had the post-tour blues—whatever you want to call it.

Usually, I can shake it by just doing some work in my studio. Up until that time I always thought of my studio as my sanctuary— a place to jam and clear my head. But, for the first time, it didn't seem that way. I just didn't have the desire to play at all. In fact, I was so fried I wondered whether I was ever going to be able to write anything again. So, I just simply let go. Then, boom, one day, all of a sudden the desire came back.

I think I learned something important. There are really three parts to the creative process. First there is inspiration, then there is the execution, and finally there is the release. The last part is more important than I ever realized. And after the last tour, I didn't allow myself to cleanse before I jumped back in, and it really screwed me up for a while.

CORGAN: One of the things that struck me after listening to all your albums is your fearlessness—you've never been afraid to go where you've wanted to go. You've played blues, you've played crazy music, you've played synthesizer music...

VAN HALEN: I think my desire to do my own thing came from my dad. He was a real soulful guy. He played sax and clarinet like a motherfucker. Unfortunately, he was also an alcoholic who died when he was 66. But he lived a full life. My mom, on the other hand, is 80, but she doesn't live. So I'm trying to find a balance between them. I don't want to be like my mom and live to be 80, and not live. And I don't want to die at 66 like my dad.

CORGAN: You created the sound of Van Halen. After all these years, how do you confront your own legacy? Do you ever worry about repeating yourself?

VAN HALEN: Not really. Change is a natural part of my evolution as a player. It just happens, because everybody changes over a period of time. It's a very unconscious thing. I think the unreleased acoustic piece I just played you before the interview sounds different from anything I've ever done, yet I didn't sit down and say, "I have to do something different."

CORGAN: I admire your attitude, because I feel like I'm always fighting not to repeat myself.

VAN HALEN: I don't know. Every time I walk into the studio it seems like the first time. It's like I've never written a song before. I am just as scared. In fact, someone asked me the other day, what I thought I had learned about making music after all these years, and I said, "Nothing." I'm scared shitless all the time. I'm really insecure that way.

CORGAN: At what age did you start playing guitar?

VAN HALEN: I started smoking, drinking and playing the guitar at age 12.

CORGAN: And how old were you when you recorded your first album?

VAN HALEN: I was 22.

CORGAN: So how did you get from playing your first open G chord to playing "Eruption"?

VAN HALEN: Practice. I used to sit on the edge of my bed with a six-pack of Schlitz Malt talls. My brother would go out at 7 P.M. to party and get laid, and when he'd come back at 3 A.M., I would still be sitting in the same place, playing guitar. I did that for years—I still do that.

CORGAN: But where did that attack style of playing come from? At 22, you were *killing* people.

VAN HALEN: I have no idea. I can tell you how I came up with certain techniques, but the rest is a mystery. It's the way I learned to communicate, because I was never very good with words. I was just chosen.

CORGAN: I find it interesting that it was so unpremeditated.

VAN HALEN: I believe that every one on this planet is born with a gift, and I was just lucky enough to find mine. So I'm very blessed, and very grateful.

CORGAN: So, what was it like to wake up and find you were suddenly everybody's guitar hero?

VAN HALEN: It was weird. But I'll tell you what was even weirder. Before our first record came out, this guy wrote an article about the band in one of the major Los Angeles newspapers. He singled me out as the important member. He just raved about my playing and didn't really say much about Roth. And it freaked David out because he was the lead singer and frontman. It really upset him that I was getting the attention.

I kind of felt bad and really didn't know what to do. It was like this journalist almost ruined the band and my life by praising my work. He actually hurt me by putting the spotlight on me. I was like, "Fuck you, just let me play." The tension it created in the band was unbelievable. I was like, "Holy shit, David! What did I do wrong? Did I play too good? I'll play worse. Will that make you happy?"

CORGAN: Yeah, suddenly everyone was tapping and doing whammy-bar dives. What was that like?

VAN HALEN: Actually, I thought it was kind of funny. Because, with me, it was a form of expression—part of my style. When I used the stuff I invented, I was telling a story, while I felt that the people who were imitating me were telling a joke. I felt other players tended to use tapping and false harmonics as a trick, instead of incorporating them into their vocabulary.

CORGAN: On your debut album, *Van Halen* [*1978*], your guitar solo, "Eruption," was the second track. Wasn't it kind of a bold move to place this crazy guitar instrumental so close to the beginning of the record? Was it a conscious move?

VAN HALEN: The whole story behind "Eruption" is unusual. It wasn't even supposed to be on the album. I showed up at the recording studio early one day and started to warm up because I had a gig on the weekend and I wanted to practice my solo guitar spot. Our producer, Ted Templeman, happened to walk by and he asked, "What's that? Let's put it on tape!" So I took one pass at it, and they put it on the record. I didn't even play it right. There's a mistake at the top end of it. To this day, whenever I hear it I always think, "Man, I could've played it better."

CORGAN: But what was the idea behind making it the second track? It certainly gave it more weight than if you had sequenced it at the end of the album.

VAN HALEN: I think they put it there because it was different, but I'm not really sure. At that point in my career, I really didn't have any control over anything. I was just like, "Yes, sir. Whatever."

We barely had any input in the early days of the band. I mean, there are so many things wrong with those early records—the drums sound like shit on the first album and the bass is barely audible. We just played live, they recorded it, and it got put out.

CORGAN: How did you guys write the first album? It's my guess that much of your early music evolved out of jamming.

VAN HALEN: A lot of the basic ideas were things that I came up with when I used to practice on the edge of my bed. I would take those ideas to band practice. At the time, we were rehearsing in David's father's basement, so me and Alex [*Van Halen, drums*] would go over there by ourselves and jam on the ideas for hours until we came up with something we were happy with. For example, Al and I jammed on the basic riff from "And the Cradle Will Rock" two hours a day for two straight weeks. [*laughs*] We didn't really know what to do with it, but we were having fun because it just sounded so wicked. Then, out of nowhere, the chorus came to us and it was finished.

Sometimes you really have to work for inspiration. But ultimately, it's not really work, because my brother and I genuinely love to jam. I'd say that's the way most things happen in our band. It usually begins with me and Al, which is funny in a way, because most people don't usually think of the guitar and drums as a unit. It's usually bass and drums.

CORGAN: But I think that's the way a band *should* be constructed— the core of a band should be built on the relationship between the guitarist and the drummer. It's the simpatico relationship between me and our drummer, Jimmy Chamberlain, that provides the foundation for the Pumpkins. Drums can do so much more than just hold down the groove.

VAN HALEN: Exactly. I think Al's drumming is more musical because he listens to me rather than just being concerned with maintaining a steady groove. Billy, how do you write with the Pumpkins?

CORGAN: It's close to how you do it. I'm definitely responsible for coming in with some basic chord changes, or ideas. Everybody in the band looks to me to come up with the basic seed, so it's not very productive to come in with nothing.

VAN HALEN: It's the same with us! You know, it's like, "Well, watcha got, Ed?"

CORGAN: Yeah! And if you don't have anything, everybody will stand around and look at their watches and say things like, "This is boring. Uh, can I go? I got a date tonight."

On the other hand, you can't do it yourself. I'll come in with a string of riffs, and direct the musical ideas. But you still need a band and their input to make the ideas come alive. You can't underestimate band chemistry. You still need that—it's that weird jelling of people.

One of the cool things about Van Halen is that you've always been able to write great hit singles. Unlike other hard rock bands, you never shied away from writing pop music.

VAN HALEN: Again, I just go with whatever comes out. I can't help the fact that I've written "Can't Stop Loving You" or "Jump." Don't blame me. [*laughs*] Actually, if I could deliberately sit down and write a pop hit, all my songs would be pop hits!

Let's put it this way. I play what I like to hear. And sometimes I like to hear something poppy, and sometimes I don't.

CORGAN: *Van Halen II* [*1979*] is a really good record, but it sounds to me like you really didn't have the time to fully explore all your guitar and song ideas.

VAN HALEN: It was very hurried. We had just toured for a year, and we only had two weeks to write and record. But I'll never forget the questions we got after the second record was released: "Why does this record sound different from the first album?" Because it's not the first album! It's always a Catch-22 situation. They hate you if you're the same, and they hate you if you're different.

CORGAN: But you agree that it wasn't completely realized?

VAN HALEN: Yeah, but I don't think it was because of us. There was a lot of cocaine on the console—and it wasn't necessarily the band's. That was a problem. And we weren't allowed any input on the mix.

But ultimately we were just plain rushed. That's why you hear that little riff fade out at the end of the album—Al and I didn't want to stop. [*laughs*] We weren't done, but we had a deadline.

CORGAN: I think two great albums are *Women and Children First* [*1980*] and *Fair Warning* [*1981*].

VAH HALEN: I was starting to get more involved.

CORGAN: And it shows.

VAN HALEN: Especially on *Fair Warning*. But what I had to do to get involved was very strange. We'd work during the day, and I wasn't very happy with the way things were going or the way people were approaching the whole recording process. I would sneak back into the studio at 4 A.M. with Donn Landee, the engineer, and completely re-record all the solos and overdubs the way I wanted them. The fucked-up thing was, no one even noticed. That's how uninvolved they were on a musical level.

CORGAN: *Fair Warning* is a really mean, dark album. That was unusual for you guys. Up until that time you were more of a party band.

VAN HALEN: It was kind of a dark period in my life. I was getting married, which flipped Roth out to the bone. I actually overheard him say, "That fucking little prick, not only is he winning all the guitar awards, but he's also the first to marry a movie star." So that's what I was up against. A guy that wanted everything that was going my way. The funny thing was, I really didn't want the attention, and it came to me anyway. I didn't want the press—it was like, "Leave me alone."

CORGAN: Let's talk about some of the specifics of *Fair Warning*. What can you tell me about "Push Comes to Shove"?

VAN HALEN: That was Roth's idea of trying to cash in on the reggae thing. I said, "Okay, if you want that kind of beat, I'll see what I can do."

CORGAN: That song has an incredible guitar solo.

VAN HALEN: I'll never forget that one. We were sitting in the studio with our producer, Ted Templeman, and I knew exactly what I wanted to do. I must have played that solo over 20 times, and Ted kept saying, "No, it's not good enough." So I said, "Okay, but I don't understand what you want." So we just called it a day. Later that night I came back and played the same solo that I played 20 times that day and left it. The next day he heard it and said, "That's great."

On the whole album I was angry, frustrated and loose. It's like the solo in "Unchained." I love that song. It's rare that I can listen back to my own playing and get goose bumps, but that's one of them.

My frustration continued to grow when we made our next album, *Diver Down* [*1982*]. Half that album was damn cover tunes, and I hated every minute of making it. David Lee Roth had the idea that if you covered a successful song, you were half way home.

C'mon—Van Halen doing "Dancing in the Streets"? It was stupid. I started feeling like I would rather bomb playing my own songs than be successful playing someone else's music.

Ultimately, that's why I built the studio we're now standing in. I built it so I could work on my music without having to battle anybody. So after *Diver Down* I demanded that we do *1984* [*1984*] in my own studio, my way. The motivation behind *Diver Down*—which was to play it safe and make money—was completely different from *1984*. One had heart where the other was bullshit. *Diver Down* is my least favorite record—even though I still tried to put myself into it.

CORGAN: That's so strange, because a studio devoted to the band seems like such a positive thing.

VAN HALEN: That's what I would've thought. But I was trying to take the band in a direction that I thought was appropriate, and Roth was trying to take the band in more of a Las Vegas direction. And there he is.

CORGAN: You did what you felt was right and it succeeded. I ran into similar obstacles recently. I met with a lot of resistance when I wanted our newest album [Mellon Collie and the Infinite Sadness (*Virgin*)] to be a double CD. Many people thought I was going to ruin the band by doing it. But it proved to be the right thing.

VAN HALEN: You have to follow your heart. But don't ever get cocky and say to yourself, "Hey, I was right." Just do what you feel. Do you understand what I mean?

CORGAN: Yes, you can't gloat.

VAN HALEN: Right. When "Jump" went Number One, I was almost embarrassed. You did this double album because it's what you wanted to do, not because you wanted to prove anybody wrong or make money.

CORGAN: In the beginning, though, I have to admit that I did have a chip on my shoulder. I did want to prove everyone wrong. But after I went through the process and came out the other side, I realized why I had to do it. It wasn't about anyone else. In fact, the deeper I get into my life as a musician, I'm discovering that it becomes less and less about other people, and more about what I want to do. And that's a good place to be.

So I can understand what you're talking about. There are all these fish swimming around you, and their motivation is not necessarily to make sure that you're playing great or that you're going have a great show that night. Instead, it's, "Are there people in the fucking seats?"

VAN HALEN: The thing is, after 20 years it doesn't change! I hope you're prepared for that. [*laughs*]

CORGAN: I read in *Van Halen II*'s liner notes that you guys once parachuted into a stadium show. [*laughs*] What was that all about?

VAN HALEN: That was one of Roth's big ideas. I'm not even sure why, but he said, "Let's parachute into the stadium." Of course we couldn't do it ourselves, so we hired four professional sky divers to jump out of an airplane right before our set. The idea was that we would wear identical gear and run on stage and pretend it was us that jumped out of the plane. So there we were, wearing these crazy, heavy outfits, sweating our balls off, waiting for the sky divers to come down so we could jump on stage. It was so silly, and it almost turned into a complete catastrophe, because while we were trying to get out of the gear, Al severely twisted his ankle and had to play the show with practically a broken foot.

I guess that's why Dave's in Vegas. He saw playing music as show biz, and it's not show biz to me. I should've known when Roth said, "Let's say we're two years younger than we really are." And I'd say, "Why? I'm only 22. What's the difference?" That still causes problems for me to this day. I'm 41, and people think I'm 39.

CORGAN: But in a positive light, it sure made things interesting in an incredibly dull period of music.

VAN HALEN: Hey, we were young and crazy. We were trying to do all the things that Led Zeppelin did—throw televisions out the window, and so on. We used to drive people crazy. For example, very early on, we were on a tour supporting Journey. They would never give us soundchecks and treated us like shit in general, so we liked to fuck with them anyway we could. So while they were on stage we would sneak in and destroy their rooms—we'd use fire hoses and extinguishers, whatever we could get our hands on.

What really drove them crazy was that at the beginning of the tour no one knew who we were. The audience would say, "What the fuck is this?" But by 30 dates into the tour, we were the ones selling the tickets. In fact, halfway through the tour we wanted to bail, and despite all the shitty stuff we did to them, they begged us to stay on. Needless to say, we didn't. [*laughs*]

Here's another good story from that tour: We were in Madison, Wisconsin, and while I was out of my room, Al and David snuck in and grabbed my table and chairs, took out the screen and threw them out the window. When I came back to my room I was like, "Where the hell is my table?" So I looked out my window and there, seven stories down, were my chair and table lying in the snow. The screen had totally disappeared.

I figured it must have been Roth, so I went down to the desk and said, "My name is David Lee Roth, can I have the key to my room?" I went into his room, grabbed the table and chair and put them in mine. When the cops came, they looked in my room and said, "Hey, there's no screen here but there's a table and chair. Then they looked in Roth's room and said, "Hey, there's no table and chair here, but the screen is intact." They couldn't figure it out. [*laughs*]

CORGAN: I saw the *1984* tour. In fact, I waited in line all night and froze my ass off to get tickets, and I was on your side of the stage, of course. It struck me that the band seemed really disjointed at that point in time.

VAN HALEN: Well, yeah. It had degenerated into the "Johnny Carson Show." There were so many solo spots that it seemed like we were doing the show one person at a time. We were never out there as a band for more than 10 minutes.

CORGAN: Yeah, it was pretty strange. David would tell some jokes, and you would disappear off to the side of the stage and go off into "Eddie's House."

VAN HALEN: It was like, "Hey, Johnny, are you done with your monologue yet?" It wasn't a band anymore. It couldn't have gone on that way. It was a good thing that Roth quit.

CORGAN: Is it strange to you that even though you were going through so much turmoil behind the scenes around the time of *1984*, your public image was still so positive and uplifting?

VAN HALEN: Roth was very good at maintaining the public persona of the band. That was his thing. It's strange, because we're still perceived as a party band, and I still never go out and party. I guess that has to do with Sammy.

CORGAN: But there's nothing wrong with the fact that your music makes people feel good.

VAN HALEN: That's my point. The music makes people feel good. I'm not sure if it's our responsibility to also act the part. The point I'm trying to make is that at this point in my life I would like to strive for something deeper. There are more emotions I would like to express, that are difficult to express when you are perceived as a "party band."

CORGAN: So do it. Do it, and take your lumps. I have almost the opposite problem. I'm viewed as this weird, crippled character. [*laughs*] So it's not always easy to know that people view you as this overly emotional, overly sensitive big guy. But artist to artist, you've got to take your lumps.

VAN HALEN: Oh, I know, and I do. Hey, c'mon man, I've been at this for over 25 fucking years. I've taken them! There's a plaque on our wall that says we've sold over 65 million albums, and I don't feel I've accomplished anything. I feel like I'm just getting started.

CORGAN: That's the artist in you speaking. Even in your guitar hero days, you never sucked up the vain glory of it. The band has never appeared snooty or snotty. And I think that's why your fan base is big. You guys never went through that "sick period" that a lot of bands who've recorded for 20 years often go through, where they hit rock bottom with their fans. Even around *Diver Down*, which admittedly is not your strongest effort, people were still there for you. And I think that says a lot about you personally. That you care, you want to have a good time, and you want others to have a good time.

VAN HALEN: And I think there's a certain amount of honesty and heart and soul that goes into it that people can feel, even on *Diver Down*.

CORGAN: That's why you'll always have people on the other end for you.

VAN HALEN: Music is for people. The word "pop" is simply short for popular. It means that people like it. I'm just a normal jerk who happens to make music. As long as my brain and fingers work, I'm cool.

Michael Sexton

GUITAR WORLD, DECEMBER 1996

ERUPTIONS

Dave isn't the one, Sammy's cryin', and Eddie's hot for Gary. Right now, life seems pretty complicated for Van Halen.

By Steven Rosen
Licensed from International Features Agency

ONE OF THE first things you notice upon entering the maintenance room of Edward Van Halen's 5150 complex is a series of five Polaroid snapshots, arranged vertically along the edge of a doorway. Four of these depict Edward sitting atop a 5150 combo amp, grinning aimlessly, as if the photographer was simply testing the settings on the camera. The fifth picture captures the band—Edward, brother Alex, Michael Anthony and Sammy Hagar—in cozy, smiling camaraderie, their arms draped around each other's shoulders. Most striking about this print, however, is the fact that someone has plunged a yellow push pin through Hagar's face. The perfect placement of the pin indicates that the deed was about as accidental as the assassination of Lincoln. No, this is nothing but bad Van Halen voodoo, mean mojo stuff—an act of venom and doom.

By now, only the brain dead are unaware of the changes that have rocked the Van Halen camp. Singer Sammy Hagar is gone, his solid gold locks nothing but a memory. David Lee Roth, absent for over a decade, returned to appear on a pair of new tracks available on the band's *Best of Volume 1* greatest hits package, the band's first such compilation ever. But despite feverish speculation that the flamboyant singer would rejoin Van Halen, fate and, in all likelihood, Eddie deemed otherwise: Roth is out, history for the second time. Of course, Van Halen had a powerfully felt reason to reject a reunion that would, if nothing else, have been a diamond-studded cash cow for the group.

"We're from different planets; we don't communicate," says Eddie of Roth. "We just don't see things the same way. I'm not saying that he's a bad person at all—I actually fuckin' love the guy. But I don't need that kind of negative energy around me. I don't know how to explain it, but Dave kinda sucks the life out of me." So instead of David Lee Roth making a dramatic re-entry into the Van Halen fray, a dark horse candidate emerged and was handed one of rock's plum jobs outright—none other than the former Extreme frontman, Gary Cherone. Cherone, known for his acrobatic stage antics and extraordinary vocal range, impressed Eddie with his quiet manner: "He's like a brother. He's shy, he's a quiet guy and has no fuckin' attitude. He's just a beautiful human being. Plus, the guy sings and sounds like an angel."

Van Halen, who despises the politics of the music business as much as Roth revels in it, has, these past few uncertain months, endured a romp through hell without sunscreen. In an intimate conversation which initially began at his Hollywood Hills hideaway and three days later ended with a frantic game of phone tag, he shared with *Guitar World* his view of Van Halen's massive implosion, the too public upheaval that led to the ousting of one lead singer and the temporary resurrection of another. He also talked about the band's recent greatest hits album, a work which in its depth reveals just how much rock's premier guitarist matured as an artist and as a man, in the course of 20 spectacular, if turbulent, years.

GUITAR WORLD: The last few months have been difficult ones for the band.

EDWARD VAN HALEN: Yeah, the last three months have been a full plate—and a few desserts I didn't plan on ordering. There had been a variety of conflicts brewing between Sammy and the band since I quit drinking on October 2, 1994. Then things really came to a head when we began work on the soundtrack to the movie *Twister*. It got so bad that I actually started drinking again.

GW: What were some of the more nagging issues?

VAN HALEN: Well, in the last couple of years, Sammy went through a lot of changes; he divorced his wife of 23 years and, possibly because of that, stopped being a team player. He was especially irritated by the fact that I began to get involved with the lyric writing. Sammy would say, "You never complained about the lyrics before!" Well, I wasn't sober before, and I wasn't even listening to the lyrics!

It's not like I suddenly wanted Sammy to be my puppet or anything, but once in a while, I would take issue with a specific lyric or line. For example, I always hated the words to "Wham, Bam Amsterdam," from *Balance*, because they were all about smoking pot—they were just stupid. Lyrics should plant some sort of seed for thought, or at least be a little more metaphorical.

GW: So you really began to have problems with Sammy around the time of making *Balance*?

VAN HALEN: I'd say that we actually had problems on every album except for *5150*. Sammy wouldn't even work with Andy Johns on *For Unlawful Carnal Knowledge*; he demanded to work with Ted Templeman, because Ted lets him get away with everything.

Then, like I said, things got really ridiculous when we started working on the music for *Twister*. Alex had called up the director, Jan De Bont, to ask him how closely he wanted the lyrics of the song that became "Humans Being" to be related to the content of the movie. De Bont said, "Oh, please don't write about tornadoes. I don't want this to be a narrative for the movie."

So we put him in contact with Sam, who called me and said, "I had a great conversation with De Bont and everything is cool." Then—maybe two seconds after I got off the phone with Sammy—De Bont rang me up and was like, "Uh, Sammy is a little strange. I kept telling him that he shouldn't write any lyrics about tornadoes, but he still kept insisting that I fax him tornado-related technical jargon. Does Sammy just want to learn about twisters for his own personal reasons?" I said, "Beats the hell out of me." And so what lyrics did Sammy come back with? "Sky is turning black, knuckles turning white, headed for the hot zone." It was total tornado stuff! Not only did Alex and I tell him not to do that, but the director of the fucking movie told him, "Do not write about tornadoes."

We had the music for the song completely done for six weeks, during which time Sammy had refused to fly to the studio from Hawaii, and suddenly the deadline was on us and we had no lyrics. So I was on the spot, and I came up with the title "Humans Being" and a melody. When Sammy finally decided to show, he, [*producer*] Bruce Fairbairn and I ended up writing the lyrics together at the last minute. Sammy sang the track in an hour, because he had an eight o'clock flight to catch. Sammy was long gone to wherever when I came up with the low, growling vocal part which I sang, "We're just humans/humans being," and he never heard any of that until the record came out. That's how into it he was.

The situation with Sammy was so bad that I had to warn Bruce not to let him know that I had come up with the title and the melody, because if he had found that out he would have completely turned off. Whenever I suggested something to Sammy, he would just stop listening to me.

GW: There were a lot of rumors circulating that Sammy was unhappy with the band because he felt he was being forced into projects he didn't want any part of.

VAN HALEN: Sammy was dead against the greatest hits package, because he was afraid it would lead to comparisons between him and David Lee Roth. I said, "Wait a fuckin' minute, Sammy, this band . has been putting out records for 20 years and never put out a greatest hits—but you already have two of them [Best of Sammy Hagar, *1992*; Unboxed, *1994*]!

It just goes to show you that in his mind, he was always a solo artist—once a solo artist always a solo artist. He was only into being in Van Halen for the prestige of it.

GW: You've recently begun collaborating with super-producer Glen Ballard [*Alanis Morissette, Aerosmith*], who co-wrote the two new songs on *Best of Volume 1*.

VAN HALEN: Glen is just the most beautiful guy you'll ever meet. I won't work with anybody else any more—there's no reason to. He and I connect, like musical soul mates. He wrote Alanis Morissette's album in one day, and he and I are that way, too. When we get together, we brainstorm and a song is done in two seconds.

GW: What was Sammy's reaction when you started working with Glen?

VAN HALEN: We had several band meetings with Sammy where we told him that if he wanted to continue with Van Halen, he had to stop running around doing all his solo shit and become more of a team player—which might involve collaborating on a lyrical level. He said, "No problem." We had another meeting to reiterate that after the premiere of *Twister*.

So right after that, we began working on this song "Between Us Two," because we thought it had amazing potential. Sammy Called Mike [*Anthony, bass*] one Sunday afternoon and said, "I heard that Glen has some great ideas for the song. I'm really excited." Then he called me Sunday evening to give me his fax number so I could fax over Glen's lyrics. And then, suddenly, in the middle of giving me the number, he just started yelling and screaming at me: "This is a fucking insult! I ain't gonna sing someone else's bullshit!" I was totally startled, like, "Wait a minute, we discussed this at length on two occasions. We didn't spring this on you, man." Finally I said, "Okay, forget the new lyrical treatment, but at least come down, take another pass at the performance and change a few lines." He just answered, "Yeah, well, whatever."

That's when I finally put my foot down. I said, "Sammy, if you're not here at the studio by six o'clock tomorrow, don't ever bother coming back." The next day, he showed up like nothing had ever happened—like he hadn't yelled and screamed at me. Did he think I was some idiot who didn't remember what had happened the night before? I'm sober now, dude.

Glen and I were sitting there working on the song, and the opening line was something like, "I want to see you/I want to know who you are"—kind of a *Dark Side of the Moon* vibe, the premise being, "I want to touch your soul, I want to get to know you." Then Sammy decided to change it to some shit like, "I can't see your diamond ring/through your shining star." I was like, "Sam, please, Glen's got some great lyrics here, just go with them." His only reply was, "If I thought those lyrics were better, I would sing them...besides I have a plane to catch." And he just left. Glen and I were dumfounded. Then Glen asked me, "How long has this been going on?" I said, "Longer than I'd care to mention."

So anyway, that was the last straw. I called Sammy a bunch of times and, when he finally returned my call, I said, "Sam, if you want to make another record or do another tour, you've gotta be a team player. Van Halen is a band—not the Sammy Hagar show, or the Eddie Van Halen, Alex Van Halen or Michael Anthony show. We could be called Piss for all I care, but we are a band."

So I went over this shit like 11 times with him, and he finally said, "Yeah, goddamnit, I'm fuckin' frustrated. I want to go back to being a solo artist." And I said, "Thank you for being honest."

We ended up hanging up like everything was cool because it was all out in the open. He'd admitted that he wanted to do solo stuff. And I said, "Well, you can't be in a band and that, too, so see ya." I didn't fire him—he quit.

I'll put it very simply: Dave and Sam both suffer from L.S.D.: lead singer disease. Except Dave never lied.

GW: Speaking of David Lee Roth, how did he come back into the picture?

VAN HALEN: Dave happened to call me around the same time Sammy quit, because Warner Bros. had notified him that the greatest hits package was going to come out, and he had a few questions about the packaging and other details like that. I told him, "Dave, I really don't know yet, I'll call you mid-week and let you know." We were on the phone for about 45 minutes and we apologized for things we had said back in high school—even junior high. It was probably one of the best conversations I've ever had with him. Especially since as long as I've known him, we were never really friends. We were just from different planets. But band-wise, it just seemed to work.

A few days later, instead of calling David with the information on the CD, I decided to drive over to his house. I told him that the basic idea was to do a single CD that would be half him and half Sammy. That was another big problem we had with Sammy, by the way; he wanted to have more of his songs on the greatest hits than Dave's.

GW: What was it like going to Dave's house that first time?

VAN HALEN: We just had a great time bullshitting as friends. We hung out for about three hours and smoked some cigars. It was only about two weeks later, when I realized that the only new track we had for the greatest hits was "Humans Being," that I came up with the crazy idea of having Dave sing on a couple of new songs. We thought about it for a couple of days and said, "Yeah, why the fuck not?" So I called Dave and said, "Would you be interested?" and he said "Sure, I'm not doing anything." I was very clear that he was not in the band—that it was just a project. What I wanted to do was write five new songs and pick two out of those five.

We had a little bit of a difficult time because we wrote a song for him that he didn't particularly care for. It wasn't up his alley. So we got past that and Glen Ballard and I sat down with Dave, and I played him all this new material I had. Eventually we narrowed it down to this pop song, "Me Wise Magic," and a shuffle, "Can't Get This Stuff No More," with a "Panama" sort of groove. "Me Wise Magic" has a line in it, "I know what you're thinking," which Dave felt uncomfortable with. He said, "That bit sounds so angry; it's just not me. People want to hear Dave sing." But I thought it was majestic; it takes you on a roller coaster because there are so many changes. I nicknamed it "The Three Faces of Shamus" because there is that first low part, the high part and then the chorus. All three have completely different vibes going on. At first he wasn't into that one at all. A week later I was still playing him songs and finally he said, "What about that first one?" So, finally, he came around and realized it wasn't as dark and angry as he originally thought.

During this process, Dave and I were really becoming good

friends. In my heart I really wanted to believe that he had changed a bit. We worked and we worked, and he actually thanked me for hanging in there with him. It was a struggle to find anything that would inspire him and that he could connect to. Finally we came up with the other song and Glen suggested the title and the premise of it. So Dave came up with the lyrics and it worked. But Dave said, "Thanks, because anyone else would have probably thrown their arms up and said fuck it." And I said, 'Well you're a trooper, however long it takes and whatever. It's about making it a good song. There's no time frame here, it doesn't have to be done tomorrow. I just wanted to find something you liked and I'm glad I found one."

GW: So the two of you were able to put all of your past acrimony behind you?

VAN HALEN: Oh, yeah, we were actually becoming friends. Before we went to the MTV Video Awards, we all sat down—[*Van Halen manager*] Ray Daniels, Dave, Al, Mike and I—because we knew we were going to get mobbed by the press. And it was actually Dave who said, "Let's tell the truth." Less to remember. And the truth is, we did two songs for the best-of, we did two videos, and that's it.

We could go out there and make a killing on tour with Roth, but we're not a nostalgia band. I would never just take somebody's money for playing old songs to bring back memories. Memories are memories to be left memories. If we ever did that with Roth, we'd have to write and record a new record and then play a few of the old ones. I'm sure a lot of fans would love to see it—but some things, like I said, are better left to memory.

GW: So why aren't you making a new record with David? Was there some sort of fracture?

VAN HALEN: Everything went to pieces at the MTV Video Awards. After we went out on stage to present the award to Beck, we started doing some interviews there, and I was just telling the truth—the way it is. I said, "If we do a tour we'll have to write and record—a new record. But before any of that can happen, I have hip replacement scheduled for December 16, and that's going to put me out of commission for at least four to six months.

After doing a couple of these interviews, Dave's attitude changed. I asked him what was wrong, and he said, "Well, what's with this hip thing? Would you stop mentioning the hip thing?" I said "Okay, no problem. In the next interview I won't say a word about my hip." He turned to me and said, "You fuckin' better not." And man, I lost it! I yelled, "You motherfucker, don't ever talk to me or anybody like that again. Don't bother calling me anymore."

I thought he had changed, but two minutes on stage and a half-assed standing ovation and he turned right back into the old Dave that I hated.

GW: Who chose the tracks for the *Best of Volume 1*?

VAN HALEN: Ray and Al came up with a list and I just looked at them and said, "Yeah, fuck, I don't care." Because there's a second volume ready to go. There are a ton of other songs that people get pissed about when we don't play them live.

GW: In previous interviews, you've said that you didn't want to do a greatest hits album.

VAN HALEN: I changed my mind. What's wrong with that? Valerie [*Bertinelli, Edward's wife*] is always on the Internet, and for a lot of the people out there, their first exposure to the band was *Balance*. And when they find out we have 10 other albums, they're not gonna go out and buy 'em all. So why not put a package together so they can at least get a taste and a history of the band? Next year will be the 20th anniversary of the recording of our first record, so I don't see a problem with putting out a greatest hits record—not as long as the next record we make is great.

GW: What gear setup did you use on the most recent tracks?

VAN HALEN: The meat and the beef of the sound is the 5150. And I did experiment with some new stuff—I used a talk box on "Can't Get This Stuff No More," but Matt [*Bruck, Van Halen's guitar tech*] actually ran it for me. My mouth wasn't big enough or something because when I tried it just sounded like a wah-wah. I played and then we added it later with Matt doing it through a re-amp or whatever you call it. On "Me Wise Magic" I'm using the prototype Peavey with the Steinberger tremolo.

GW: During the period when you were in vocalist hell, did you think about maybe putting together a solo album of some sort?

VAN HALEN: No, not at all. A long time ago, when Dave totally took us by surprise and just quit, we didn't audition anybody. It was Sammy and that was it. We were just excited to have somebody who was into singing. Actually, my plan at the time—and I wouldn't necessarily have called it a solo record because Mike and Al would have played on it—was to get Mike Rutherford [*Genesis*], Pete Townshend, Phil Collins and Joe Cocker, all of whom I had talked to. I had written "Right Now" back then and I wanted Joe Cocker to sing on it. It would have been fucking great. That's what I wanted to do, write a record where I did all the music and had a different singer on each song. Logistically, it would have been a nightmare—people on tour, contractual agreements, companies pissing and moaning—and we'd probably only be finishing it now. It would have been fun. Hopefully, in the future I'll still be able to do that.

GW: Looking at *Best of Volume 1*, which provides sort of a capsule view of what Van Halen has done, makes me think: Did you have any sense 20 years ago of the volume of music you would create? Could you see down the road at all?

VAN HALEN: Believe it or not, since I've gotten sober I don't think I've done shit. I don't think I've done anything. I feel like I'm just starting.

GW: You say you feel like you've just begun, but the truth is, Van Halen is one of the few guitar-driven rock bands to still exist here in the Nineties. Most of the other bands who were around and thriving in the Eighties are gone.

VAN HALEN: Let's just call us a rock and roll band. We just are what we are. I don't know how to explain it, we survived punk the first time around, we survived disco and grunge and rap and whatever. We're a rock and roll band and we just do what we do.

GW: Do you have any opinions about the other guitar-driven groups out there—Metallica, maybe, or Soundgarden or any others?

VAN HALEN: I don't really listen to people. I like singers. I like Peter Gabriel, I love Chris Cornell, I like Tori Amos, the guy from Bush. I thought Kurt Cobain was fucking incredible. And Billy Corgan I like.

GW: When you did that cover story with Corgan [*Guitar World, April 1996*], did you feel a connection with him?

VAN HALEN: Oh, yeah, because he's probably one of the few citizens of the alternative nation, or whatever you want to call it, that admits Van Halen was an influence. Everyone else says Kiss. I mean, give me a fuckin' break. If they play guitar, they must have heard Van Halen somewhere down the line. I just don't see Kiss being a guitar-inspiring type of thing. I mean, I'm not putting Kiss down at all, I love Gene [*Simmons*], he helped us out in the beginning and without him we probably wouldn't be where we are. But to say Ace Frehley was the reason you picked up a guitar?

GW: Do you worry at all about what your audience will think about the changes in the band, primarily the addition of Gary Cherone?

VAN HALEN: No, because you cannot please everyone all the time. No matter who sings, someone is not gonna like it. I'm sick and tired of being controlled, and I don't want to control. I just have so much music and I want to put it out. Gary's very talented and we work very, very well together. We'll let *Best of Volume 1* run its course and then we'll put out the new shit. I don't care...if it touches one person, then it's great. I don't care if it sells millions, I don't care if it sells a tenth of the records that we've sold. It's not about that, it's for the love of music.

GUITAR WORLD, JANUARY 1997

UNCHAINED MELODIES

Eddie reflects on some of Van Halen's greatest hits.

By Steven Rosen

"I'M NOT SAYING every song is a Top 40 hit, but they're all tunes that people want to hear when we play live," says Eddie Van Halen, describing the criteria he used to choose the songs that appear on Van Halen's *Best of Volume 1.*

Eddie seems genuinely happy to be talking about his music. In fact, he seems to be happy to talk about anything other than Van Halen's recent lead singer crisis. For the uninitiated, Sammy Hagar is out, David Lee Roth is out, and ex-Extreme frontman Gary Cherone has officially been declared Van Halen's new lead vocalist.

Unfortunately, with all the wild speculation over the future of Van Halen, the true purpose of *Best of Volume 1*—to celebrate the band's brilliant past—has been obscured. To right this wrong, we asked Sir Edward, the guitar hero's guitar hero, to focus his sharp eye and dry wit on the 17 tracks featured on the first Van Halen retrospective ever.

GUITAR WORLD: Let's begin with what is perhaps rock's most famous guitar solo, "Eruption."

EDWARD VAN HALEN: That was originally just a guitar solo I performed regularly in our club days. When we were recording our first album, our producer, Ted Templeman, heard me practicing it for an upcoming gig and asked, "What the hell is that?" I said, "It's a thing I do live—it's my guitar solo." His immediate reaction was, "Shit, roll tape!" And I said, "Whatever you say, Mr. Templeman."

We did it twice and that was it. Actually, when I get up high on the neck I make a mistake, but what the hell? It was the first record I did in my life, and I didn't know I could say, "Hey, can I try it again?" I didn't know anything. I didn't even really know how to overdub. There are no overdubs except for very minimal stuff like on "Runnin' with the Devil" and "Jamie's Cryin'." The rest is just guitar panned hard left and blowin' live.

GW: What do you remember about "Ain't Talkin' 'Bout Love"?

VAN HALEN: Believe it or not, it started as a punk rock parody. I just started slamming on two chords—A minor and G—and we were having a gas! Then I said, "Wait a minute, we can really make something out of this." We actually wrote three songs in Dave's basement that day. I remember one of them was called "Bullethead"—"B-b-b-b-b-b-b-bullethead." [*laughs*] It was actually a pretty good song.

GW: It's funny you should mention that you were taking a shot at punk. In the recently published *Waiting for the Sun: The Sound of Los Angeles*, Van Halen is described as "...a hard rock/metal quartet from Pasadena who at the eleventh hour had decided against becoming a punk band." The author obviously missed the point of what you were doing.

VAN HALEN: Yeah, and so did a lot of other people. You should see the first album cover Warner Bros. designed for us—they tried to make us look like the Clash. We said "Fuck this shit!" and came up with the Van Halen logo and made them put it on the album so that it would be clear that we had nothing to do with the punk movement.

It was our way of saying, "Hey, we're just a fucking rock and roll band, don't try and slot us with the Sex Pistols thing just because it's becoming popular."

GW: What can you tell us about "Dance the Night Away"?

VAN HALEN: It ended up completely different from how I'd imagined it. When you're writing a piece of music and other people get involved, it always turns into something else. It ended up having an almost Latin flavor to it, which I don't really dig. Still, it's a nice song—a pop tune.

GW: What about "And the Cradle Will Rock"?

VAN HALEN: Oh man, that was hilarious. I spent two weeks of rehearsals just pounding out this groove on an old Wurlitzer electric piano through an MXR flanger and a stack of Marshalls. Al and I were having a cool time playing it, but the thing is I didn't have a clue where to take it. So we just kept hammering away every day for, I swear, two weeks. Finally, one chord came and it all snapped into shape. All the changes, the verse, the solo, the breakdown, all the pieces came after going nowhere for ages.

GW: Do songs often reveal themselves to you in that fashion?

VAN HALEN: Sometimes they come complete. Sometimes you have to work on 'em. Sometimes nothing comes. But one thing is for certain: You gotta keep working to enable it to come. You can't just sit around and wait for an idea to hit you, even though that tends to happen to me a lot more now that I don't drink. It's a wicked feeling when a complete piece of music comes to you. But it's not me, I'm just a vehicle—and I really believe that.

GW: The other side of that coin is that God, or whoever, decided to hitch a ride in your vehicle, as opposed to someone else's.

VAN HALEN: Oh yeah, yeah. I was chosen to do this, and the more sober I am, the clearer I am. I've been writing a lot lately. In fact, it's hard to stop—I just go and go and go. I even have a studio in the bathroom now. I have a Peavey Combo amp in there, two self-powered Genelec speakers, an Alesis 8-track digital recorder, a Linn drum machine, an AMS stereo digital delay, a DAT, a harmonizer, a cassette machine and a Mackie mixer. And a saxophone and a fretless bass. It's just a little too small to fit a keyboard in there. [*laughs*]

GW: So it's been easier to compose since you gave up drinking?

VAN HALEN: Yeah, but it wasn't easy to convince myself that it would be. I swore to this therapist that there was no way that she would ever get me to write without a few beers. Drinking was the one thing

I could count on to help me break down my inhibitions and loosen up. She said, "Give me 12 hours." I said, "You're wasting your time, it ain't gonna work." Then she had me do some yoga and some meditation and some chanting. And then we went outside and did a bunch of weird exercises for a half-hour, to the point where I almost passed out. And then she had me sit down and relax. Next she told me to close my eyes and "imagine the room that you go to after you've had a six-pack of beer. Really try and feel that place."

I sat there for a couple of minutes and said, "Yeah, I'm kinda there." I kept my eyes closed, she handed me a guitar and I just started writing. I couldn't believe it. It took only an hour! I ended up writing five songs that day, including the music for "Me Wise Magic." It blew my mind. I just didn't want to believe I could do it without drinking.

The therapist said, "Look, you've been chosen to do this, all you're doing by drinking is blocking it. It's a lot easier for them to send it when you're clear." I just refused to believe it, but she proved me wrong. And now I can't stop writing in what I now call my "room." My wife, Valerie, recently said, "The next time you see your therapist, ask her how to get out of that 'room' and into the bedroom!" [*laughs*]

GW: Getting back to the songs: What about "Unchained"?

VAN HALEN: Ummm, what was I thinking? I don't have a clue. That whole album, *Fair Warning*, was kind of a dark period. I don't know whether it was fueled by anger or whatever, but I ended up doing 90 percent of the guitar stuff at four o'clock in the morning with our engineer, Donn Landee. Nothing was really being done during the day, so I'd go back down at night and do it.

GW: "Jump"?

VAN HALEN: That was the first song I wrote that was recorded in my home studio, 5150.

GW: It was also a very important song for the band.

VAN HALEN: Yeah, and it's a pretty well-known fact that certain people didn't want me playing keyboards because they thought I should only be a "guitar hero." But hey, I'll play Bavarian cheese whistle, if

I play it well—whatever that is.

GW: "Panama"?

VAN HALEN: It was kind of AC/DC-inspired. We had just done a tour with them the year before. It was us, Motley Crue and AC/DC in 1983, in Europe, and just the power of those guys blew my mind—the constant "boom, boom, boom." They play the same song over and over, but it's a great song. They were probably one of the most powerful live bands I've ever seen in my life. The energy...they were just unstoppable.

I'll never forget our first big tour. It was a theater-sized tour—3,000 seaters. We headlined a bill featuring Ronnie Montrose and Journey. We were supposed to do 60 shows, but we left early because we had an offer to do "Day on the Green" [*a 1995 Bill Graham concert production held in Oakland, California*]. I think Aerosmith and Foreigner were co-headlining.

We had our own trailer, and next door to us was AC/DC, who were also playing that day. Anyway, they went on before us, and I was standing on the side of the stage thinking, "We have to follow these motherfuckers?" They were so fuckin' powerful, but I remember feeling that we held our own. I was really happy. It blew my mind—I didn't think anybody could follow them.

GW: "Why Can't This Be Love?" was your first big hit with Sammy Hagar. How did that come together?

VAN HALEN: I wrote that on an Oberheim OB-8 keyboard in my bedroom. It was one of the first songs where Sammy said, "You don't mind if I follow your keyboard melody, do you?" And I said, "No, not at all," though, in general, I don't really like the vocals to follow my instrumental lines. I'd much rather have the vocal line act as counterpoint. That's why I dig Glen Ballard, who produced the two new tracks on our *Best of Volume 1* album. He's always searching for great counter lines. Our conceptual goal was to put lyrics and a melody over [*sings the first four ominous notes of Beethoven's Symphony No. 5*]. You know what I mean? What would you sing over that? But that would be the shit if it could be done. And that to me is the essence of a great and complete song: great music that stands on its own, great melodic music, great counter-vocal melody and great lyrics. And of course a good performance.

GW: Do you believe you've reached those goals on any specific track?

VAN HALEN: I don't think you ever reach complete happiness. If you do, it's done, it's over with. What I thought was the shit two years ago just doesn't have the same impact on me now. I think it's just human nature to change, to get tired of the same thing...I don't know what it is. I'm always experimenting and dicking around, but not because of any goal. Music is my life, and it's very, very hard work, which a lot of other people don't understand. It's not a nine-to-five job—it's a 25-hour-a-day job.

GW: "Dreams"?

VAN HALEN: That's the one song Mick Jones of Foreigner helped us produce. Mick was supposed to produce the whole *5150* album because Warner Bros. didn't trust us to do it on our own. But Foreigner were on the road while we were recording, so Mick really wasn't around much. So we would say, "Yeah, Mick's here producing." In the meantime, I produced Sammy's vocal and Donn and I engineered. Mick got the credit, but *5150* was really a band-produced effort.

GW: "Poundcake"?

VAN HALEN: Sometimes Al has a better ear for my playing than I do. I'll just play a hint of something, and he'll stop me and say, "That part right there." And more often than not, it will be something that will eventually evolve into a song. "Poundcake" came from Al recognizing the potential of a chord progression that I probably would have skipped over.

GW: "Right Now" was another important milestone for the band.

VAN HALEN: It took 13 years to make that record. I wrote that song a long time ago—right around the "Jump" period. Some people thought "Right Now" was really risky, but to me, it's not even stepping out. It's still a rock tune. It's just piano-based, so what the fuck? It's not a headbanger. It's not like "Poundcake" or "Judgment Day," but it's still Van Halen.

GW: If "Right Now" was considered risky, "Can't Stop Loving You" was one of your more overtly commercial songs.

VAN HALEN: Our producer at that time, Bruce Fairbairn, asked me if I had any pop ditties lying around. I had a ton of tapes, so at first I was just going to go through them to see if had anything. But I was just too lazy to dig through them all. Instead, I just decided it would be easier to write a new tune from scratch—and "Can't Stop Loving You" was the result. I played it for him and he said, "Great." I think it was one of the last things we recorded for *Balance*.

GW: What can you tell us about the new tracks with David Lee Roth? How did you compose "Me Wise Magic"?

VAN HALEN: That was just one of almost 20 songs I'd written in the previous couple of months. I played it for Dave, and at first he didn't quite care for it. Alex and I had already written a verse melody, and Dave wanted to do something where he sang more. But after playing 15 other pieces of music for him, we still couldn't find anything that inspired him.

After thinking about it, he decided he wanted to go back to "Me Wise Magic." And I went, "Okay, cool." At the time he thought it sounded angry, but I convinced him that the verse melody didn't sound angry, it just sounded like some kind of strange creature. And the chorus was undeniably majestic and powerful.

That song has major imagery for me. There are so many vibes to it; the verse is one thing, the chorus is another, the breakdown before the solo, the solo, and the whole fadeout. It's a ride!

GW: Speaking of new songs, you recently switched to Peavey after playing Music Man guitars for several years. Why the change? And can you talk a little bit about the Wolfgang guitar?

VAN HALEN: Music Man and I had a falling out. I hope there are no hard feelings. The logical place to go was Peavey because they make my amps. And I really like working with them, it's a very family-oriented place. The Wolfgang is just a natural evolution from the Music Man, 75 percent of which I designed. I just never thought that the guitar was finished. I always wanted a cross between three guitars— a Les Paul, a Telecaster and a Strat—and the Wolfgang is the realization of that dream.

To me, it's just an updated version of the Music Man. And in my opinion, if you compare them, the Wolfgang is a better guitar. It has a de-tuner on it, and the neck is angled back a bit so it's more comfortable to play. When I pick up a Music Man now it almost feels like it's bowed in. It's like playing a Les Paul and then picking up a Tele. It's a whole different feel. The neck has the same feel but the balance of the guitar is better, and I think it's better looking with the arch top. We're coming out with a tobacco sunburst, purple red, yellow, black and ivory. Six colors.

As far as the amp goes, I think the 5150 is a pretty respectable amp and, believe it or not, it's the only amp I've never blown up. You can unplug the speaker cord and keep playing and it won't blow. If you do that with a Marshall or Hi-Watt or anything else, it will just pop.

GW: You've always described your ideal guitar tone as sounding "brown." Is that still true today?

VAN HALEN: That ball has been thrown around so much that it's hard to keep track of what it originally meant. It was actually Alex's term for the sound of his snare—the meaty sound of beating on a log. It also seemed like a good way to describe my ideal sound at the time. If you listen to *Van Halen*, though, my sound is actually pretty bright—it's not really "brown" at all. It cuts.

My guitar sound is fatter these days than it is on the old records. I feel kind of guilty sometimes, because I'm definitely hogging the spectrum of sound on our records. I'm using five amps and cabinets at the same time, all with two mics on them. There's this guy in Vancouver that made me this splitter box that allows me to use six amps simultaneously. I use three 5150s for dirt and two 5150s for clean, and each amp is on a different track. Also, each amp has two mics on each cabinet, so you can change the sound of each.

GW: So you're not using Marshalls at all any more?

VAN HALEN: I use them and Hi-Watts now and then. But the meat of the sound—the beef—are the 5150s.

GW: What about the gear you use on the two new tracks? I think "Can't Get This Stuff No More" represents the first time you ever used a talk box.

VAN HALEN: Actually, Matt [*Bruck, Van Halen's guitar tech*] ran the talk box for me. My mouth wasn't big enough. I said to Glen, "You try it," because when I did it just sounded like a wah-wah. I didn't know you had to deep throat the damn thing! [*laughs*] Glen tried it first and said, "Fuck, it sounds the same as when you do it." Finally, Matt, who used one in his own band, tried it, and it sounded good.

GW: Did you use one of those Digitech Whammy pedals on the solo to "Me Wise Magic"?

VAN HALEN: No, that's just the prototype Peavey with the Steinberger tremolo. And during the end I'm using a Fernandes sustainer.

GW: What goes through your mind when you look back at all of this music?

VAN HALEN: I think it's been a hell of a ride. I think it shows growth and that we're always trying to get better at what we do. Each song is like a photograph—that's why we didn't re-mix anything. All we did was digitally remaster it so the sound quality would be better. Whatever magic was captured on each song, we wanted to leave intact.

Guitar World Presents is an ongoing series of books filled with the extraordinary interviews, feature pieces and instructional material that have made *Guitar World* magazine the world's most popular musicians' magazine. For years, *Guitar World* magazine has brought you the most timely, the most accurate and the most hard-hitting news and views about your favorite players. Now you can have it all in one convenient package: *Guitar World Presents*. The first four volumes of the series–Kiss, Van Halen, Metallica and Stevie Ray Vaughan–are here, ready to blow you away. Eddie Van Halen's fans have the opportunity to learn all about rock guitar's resident genius–straight from his mouth. Are you a Kiss fan who wants the full story behind the band's incredible 1996 reunion tour? No problem–it's all in *Guitar World Presents*, as are Stevie Ray Vaughan's tragedies and triumphs and Metallica's march to the top.

Prepare yourself. *Guitar World Presents*–the books that rock.

Guitar World Presents Kiss

From the pages of *Guitar World* magazine, the foremost musicians' publication in America, comes *Guitar World Presents Kiss*, an exciting and often explosive collection of interviews, articles and essays on rock's most famous masked marauders. In-depth conversations with band members Gene Simmons, Paul Stanley, Ace Frehley and Peter Criss chronicle the entire history of Kiss, from the band's modest beginnings in New York City to their incredible rise to international prominence, subsequent collapse and triumphant comeback on their 1996 reunion tour. Devoted Kiss fans and recent converts alike will find *Guitar World Presents Kiss* to be one book they really can't do without. Includes Photos.
Soft cover, 6"x9"–144 pages, $12.95.....00330291

Guitar World Presents Metallica

More than any other publication, *Guitar World* magazine has followed Metallica's rise from underground phenomenon to mainstream metal giant. *Guitar World Presents Metallica* features every one of the facts and figures, interviews and stories, about the band ever to have appeared in the magazine in one self-contained package. Presented in the chronological order in which they appeared in the magazine, the revealing interviews with band members James Hetfield, Kirk Hammett, Jason Newsted and Lars Ulrich tell the story of the boys from San Francisco who went on

to become the metal men of the world. Metallica fans will find everything they ever wanted to know about their heavy metal heroes right here in *Guitar World Presents Metallica*. Includes photos.
Soft Cover, 6"x9"–144 pages, $12.95.....00330292

Guitar World Presents Van Halen

No artist has ever been more closely associated with *Guitar World* magazine over the years than Edward Van Halen, the man who, in the late seventies and early eighties, changed the course of guitar history. This collection of classic interviews with the great Edward tells the real story behind his earth-shaking technique, brilliant songwriting and relationships with Van Halen's former vocalists, David Lee Roth and Sammy Hagar. This is the authoritative book about the age's seminal rock guitar god. Includes photos.
Soft Cover, 6"x9"–208 pages, $14.95.....00330294

Guitar World Presents Stevie Ray Vaughan

Stevie Ray Vaughan, bluesman, guitarist and legend, was only 35 at the time of his death, but in his lifetime he managed to revitalize the blues, influence a generation of guitarists and produce a phenomenal body of work. His story is told here in *Guitar World Presents Stevie Ray Vaughan*, a collection of articles about the great guitarist from the pages of *Guitar World* magazine. This deluxe volume features probing interviews held over the years with Stevie Ray, instructional material, a complete discography of his recorded works and living reminiscences by his fellow musicians. *Guitar World Presents Stevie Ray Vaughan* is an essential tribute to the great fallen guitar hero of our generation. Includes photos.
Soft Cover, 6"x9"–144 pages, $12.95 00330293

FOR MORE INFORMATION, SEE YOUR LOCAL MUSIC DEALER,
OR WRITE TO:

HAL•LEONARD®
CORPORATION
7777 W. BLUEMOUND RD. P.O. BOX 13819 MILWAUKEE, WI 53213

DOUBLE WHAMMY!

SUBSCRIBE NOW AND GET 'EM BOTH!